Rumer Godden was born in Sussex, England, in 1907, but was brought up chiefly in India, a country that she still regards as a second homeland. The author of ten books of fiction and non-fiction, she now lives in Buckinghamshire with her husband and two daughters, sharing with them her interest in writing, ballet, gardening, Hindu philosophy, Victorian dolls' houses, and Pekingese.

GREAT LIVES IN BRIEF
A New Series of Biographies

ACCURACY
BREVITY CLARITY
MULTUM
IN PARVO

These are
BORZOI BOOKS
Published by ALFRED A. KNOPF
in New York

HANS CHRISTIAN
ANDERSEN

"Life itself is the most wonderful fairy tale."

—HANS CHRISTIAN ANDERSEN:

The Story of My Life

Hans Christian Andersen

A GREAT LIFE IN BRIEF

BY

Rumer Godden

New York   ALFRED A. KNOPF   1955

L. C. catalog card number: 54–7218

3-1-55

THIS IS A BORZOI BOOK,
PUBLISHED BY ALFRED A. KNOPF, INC.

FIRST EDITION

In Denmark I was born, and there 'tis homely,
there clings the root whence all my being flows.
O Danish tongue, your tones are soft and comely,
none but a mother's tongue could soothe like those.
        You smiling Danish strand,
            where Viking barrows muster,
while round them orchards bloom and hop-vines
        cluster,
'tis you I love—Denmark my native land!

Oh, where is summer's boon in flowery meadow
more golden than beside this open strand?
Where falls on moonlit clover-field a shadow
so fair as in the beech's native land?
        You smiling Danish strand,
            where Dannebrog is flying—
God-gifted flag, God gave you fame undying!
'tis you I love—Denmark, my native land!

You mastered England once and overran it,
ruled all the North—but now men say you wane;
so small a land—yet up and down our planet
still ring the song and chisel of the Dane.[1]
        You smiling Danish strand,
            Plow turns up golden treasure;
God gild your future, too, in equal measure!
'tis you I love—Denmark, my native land!

---

[1] Oehlenschläger, the poet, and Thorvaldsen, the sculptor.

O land where I was born, to me so homely,
where clings the root whence all my being flows,
whose accents are my mother's, soft and comely—
no music ever stirred my heart like those.
         You smiling Danish strand,
            that swans have built their nests in,
green islands that my heart finds perfect rest in,
'tis you I love—Denmark, my native land!

ACKNOWLEDGMENTS

My thanks are due, first of all, to Dr. Topsöe-Jensen, of the University Library, Copenhagen, for his invaluable help and advice and the facilities he gave me for work at the Royal Library; to Mr. Svend Larsen and the staff at the Hans Andersen Museum, Odense; to the same Mr. Svend Larsen for permission to quote from his book on Hans Andersen; to Mr. R. P. Keigwin for permission to quote from translations of the Tales and Hans Andersen's poems; to Dr. Öve Lange, of Copenhagen, for generous help; to Messrs. Chatto & Windus for permission to use material from Dame Una Pope-Hennessy's *Charles Dickens*; to Mr. Mays, of the Public Library, High Wycombe, and Mr. Brooks, of the Central Office of Information Library, for the loan of books; to the many Danish friends I met in Denmark who went out of their way to help me.

The writer of a biography of any great man has a debt to pay to those who have written of him before. There have been many lives of Hans Christian Andersen, and I should like to make acknowledgment to them all:

Bain,

Reumert,

Mary Howitt's preface,

Jean Louis Hersholt's preface to the Collected Works,

Horace Scudder's articles,

Esther Meynell in a most delightful Hans An-dersen for boys and girls,

Svend Larsen, Director of the Museum in Odense, and

the most complete of them all, Signe Toksvig's Life of Hans Christian Andersen.

The extracts from the Tales, translated by Mr. Keigwin, are used with the permission of his pub-lishers, Flensted Forlag, of Odense. All translations from the Tales are by Mr. Keigwin with the excep-tion of *The Pen and the Inkpot.*

HANS CHRISTIAN ANDERSEN

INTRODUCTION

EVEN today Denmark is something of a fairy-tale country, with its myriad scattered islands and narrow belts of blue and silver sea, its meadows and wild marsh and heathlands, its castles and its cobbled streets and the old huddled houses that are still found in every town. Its low-beamed farmhouses with their courtyards and festival rooms seem like houses in a story, as do the manors that reflect themselves in lakes, where swans float among white lilies; the storks' nests and flaxen-haired children, the King who rides about the streets quite simply among his people, the whirling winter snowstorms and long summer nights. Like all good fairy tales, Denmark is concerned with practical things: the country's chief products are its excellent foodstuffs, and while its capital, Copenhagen, may be called the City of Flowers, of Fountains, of Smiles, it is called the City of Bicycles as well.

There is a practicability and lack of pretentiousness about the Danes that is very refreshing; as well as castles they have good hospitals and schools; the factories make beautiful things—china, silverware, and glass—besides butter, bacon, and their renowned beer. If Clive Bell's definition of civilization is right, "a sweet reasonableness and a sense of values," then surely this little nation is one of the most civilized on earth?

There are many signs of it: the courtesy that is given by everyone to everyone else; the largeness of vision and lack of possessiveness that make, for instance, co-operative farming a success; the cooking is good, always a sign, and yet the daily way of life is so simple that that of other countries seems complicated and cluttered. The visitor is struck by the number of book shops and flower shops in every town; there are few policemen in the streets, royalty can walk there without being stared at as if they were animals in the zoo. Above all, the Danes know how to play, something that seems almost to have gone out of the world; Tivoli, the big amusement park in Copenhagen, is gay with the gaiety that springs from the people, not the machine-made synthetic gaiety of fun fairs anywhere else.

This sense of fun is as lusty and fresh as the wind that blows over these small islands and flutters the scarlet and white pennants that fly on the flagpoles in almost every Danish garden; surely no land ever flew as many flags? The people seem naïvely proud and happy to be Danes.

Their history is a proud one; they are descended from the Vikings. At Elsinore on the Öresund, through which ships sail all day long, is the castle of Kronberg, and in a deep dark cellar beneath it, where no one ever goes, sleeps Holger Danske the warrior, spirit of Denmark. He is clad in steel and rests his head on his strong arms; his long beard hangs down over the marble table and has grown through it. He sleeps and he dreams and in his dreams he sees all that happens to Denmark; should real danger come, old Holger Danske will wake and the table itself will burst as he wrenches his beard from it, and the mighty blows he strikes for Denmark will be heard throughout the world. The brave spirit is still there, but the power and cruelty of the old days have mellowed to a contained security that nothing, not even the wars with Prussia, not even the long occupation from 1940 to 1945, could shake; the wars have left bitterness behind them, but it is rather the bitterness of grief than of revenge.

With all this there is something else; an elusive something under the directness and practicability, the smiles; a strange quality that is as sad and brooding as Hamlet, nostalgic, out of this world. No one, it has been said, can understand the Danes who has not experienced their summer nights, "*de lyse Nætter*," of which that inspired translator R. P. Keigwin has remarked that there is no exact translation. He says her poets are obsessed with those luminous never-dark nights, light nights, twilight nights, with their haunting eeriness.

The word "fairy" has become associated in our minds so much with children that we have forgotten its real meaning; it is from the Old French word "*faerie*" that meant "enchantment," which, in its turn, came from the Low Latin "*fata*" or "fate," something inexorable and strong. As if the northern twilight had once been inhabited by trolls, gnomes, and witches, a drop of green blood seems to be in the veins of every Danish person; and it is fitting that the most renowned of them all should be a teller of fairy tales.

On the 6th of December 1867, in the great upper room of the City Hall at Odense, the capital of Fyn, middle island of Denmark, a banquet was in process.

The guest of honor was an old man, immediately noticeable because of his height, the size of his hands and feet, his curled hair, great forehead, and wise little deepset eyes. "One was accustomed to call him ugly," a famous painter wrote, "but, in later life, his head became beautiful, a fact most people never realized." He was dressed with elegant care in black, and on his shirt front and across his breast were orders, the Swedish Order of the Knight of the Polar Star, the White Falcon of Weimar, the Red Eagle of Prussia; even from Mexico, far away across the sea, had come the Order of Our Lady of Guadalupe. He had been made a State Counselor, that strange Danish title, and by his plate lay an affectionate telegram of congratulation from the King.

On his arrival from Copenhagen the day before, he had been met by the Bishop and escorted by him to the Palace; that morning he had been given the Freedom of Odense with an illuminated charter. The town was decorated and all the schools were closed for a public holiday; now the last toast had been drunk—and Danish toasts are many—the last speech had been made, and he was asked to step to the window. It was opened and he leaned out.

The City Hall was in the Town Square with its big cobbled space lined on three sides with old houses; on the fourth side the cathedral of St. Knud, with its copper spire, rose high above everything else. That night the whole Square was illuminated; candles were burning in every house window, lanterns were at the doors; in the center of the Square was a great bonfire and round it the

Guilds came marching with torches and banners to form up in the Square; then the children came, all the children of Odense singing "In Denmark I was born," the hymn he had written for his country. It was almost too much; the flames and lights leaped up so high that they seemed to put out the stars, and the young clear voices coming up on the night air sounded like all the children of the world.

They could have been. If they had been Chinese or Japanese, African, Indian, Hebrew, Greek, American, Russian, Dutch, English, children of almost any nation, they would have known him just the same; and not only children, grownups, from kings and queens to ordinary people, from the simplest to the most gifted of every land, writers, musicians, artists, scholars. "In a little country," he had written years before, "the poet is necessarily always a poor man, therefore honor is the golden bird he tries to catch." He had added, without really believing it himself: "It remains to be seen if I can catch it by telling fairy tales."

Fairy tales! Stories for children and world-wide fame? It did not seem likely, but this was Hans Andersen.

In England and America, Andersen is something of a myth; at the mention of his name, a sentimental faraway look comes into people's eyes. "Ah yes!" they murmur, "*The Little Mermaid, Thumbelina, The Wild Swans.*" The stories seem so much a part of our heritage that we forget they were ever written and worked over, by a man who was a hard-working writer and a Dane.

Hans Andersen's countryman Kai Munk has remarked that there are two kinds of writing: writing of entertainment, which is ephemeral, and writing of existence, which has a life of its own and can be very entertaining as well. It would seem that a fairy tale must of necessity belong to the first, but Andersen's Tales are writing of existence, and potent existence at that; for all their fantasy, they are life, universal, eternal; for all their lightness of touch, they are serious.

It is difficult for us abroad to realize this, because no writer has been more mutilated by his translators. Andersen's own writing has economy and strength, an inexorableness that is sometimes so cruel that it is not for children at all; it is witty, ironical and humorous, and, though it can be intensely poignant and poetical, it is always crisp. In most translations in English this strength, this dryness, the little ironical touches are lost; he is written down, made heavy and sentimental, what the Scots call "pawky," his stories cut, the endings sometimes changed. It is a wonder that any of his quality is left.

It cannot be quite killed. We do not remember the Tales of the Grimm brothers for instance, or of Perrault, as we remember Andersen's. In the hundred-odd years since they were written, the Tales have sold more copies than any other book in the world, considering the length of time, except the Bible and Shakespeare and *Pilgrim's Progress;* there have been over two thousand editions in more than forty languages. People come from every country to his birthplace in Odense. It is heartening to think how well the enlightened little state of Denmark was repaid for the grants it gave to educate him, to let him travel, and live; those few rigsdaler have brought millions of kroner to Denmark. Men have given their lives to study him; one Japanese professor learned Danish solely to read Andersen in the original, and "Why do you need so many subjects?" asked the Indian poet Tagore on a visit to Denmark; "you need only one, Andersen."

There is a statue of Hans Andersen in the King's Garden at Copenhagen, that garden round the rich and romantic castle of Rosenborg in which, under the blowing trees—and there always seems a wind in Copenhagen —generations of children have played, hopping over the great white marble cannon balls that have edged the lawns since the sixteenth century. The statue, of Andersen reading, is so eloquent that the figure seems to speak, and on the side of the base is a scene from the tale of *The Ugly Duckling*; it is of the moment when the duckling, grown to his full size, looks into the water and sees himself a swan.

Andersen had many happy and triumphant days in his life, but none as happy as that of the illumination of Odense. A prophet is usually without honor in his own country and this was the town where he was born. He had gone shivering in his poor clothes and wooden shoes across the cobbles of the Square, had looked longingly in through the windows at the comfort and warmth inside those very houses; he had been confirmed, almost as a pauper, in the glittering St. Knud's; he was almost apprenticed to one of those Guilds, the Tailors Guild, bearing the torches below, and not far away from the windows where he stood now honored and cheered was the rough mean room that had been his home in one of the small houses of the poorest streets.

There, almost sixty years ago, an old woman had told his fortune. His father had laughed at her but to his mother she had been an oracle and a comfort, because this big ungainly boy who had such strange and delicate ideas was a worry and a puzzle; when anyone tried to think what trade he should follow as he grew up, he always said, quite simply: "I shall be famous," which was, of course, ridiculous.

But the wise woman had seemed to bear this out. "He'll have a better fortune than he deserves," she had said grudgingly; she was angry because, like his father, the boy had teased her, but she could not hold back the prediction. "He will be a wild bird who shall fly high, great and noble in the world," and then she had said: "One day the whole of Odense will be illuminated for him." His mother had repeated that everywhere and the good people had remembered it.

He stood at the window looking down. He had had, all evening, an agonizing toothache brought on by emotion and nerves; the cold December wind set it on more violently than ever; its pain was the only thing that made him feel real.

The cheers sounded in his ears, the lights and flames from the bonfire and torches leaped in the Square; important men, the Mayor, the clergy, pressed round him, his orders shone on his breast, he held the King's telegram in his hand; it seemed a long long way from that little room in the poor street.

I

HANS ANDERSEN's father and mother were so poor when they began housekeeping that they had to make most of their furniture themselves; the bed was originally a wooden frame that had been used to hold the coffin of a Count; that awed them very much; pieces of black cloth were still sticking to it, but on the 2nd of April 1805 on it, instead of a corpse, lay a living crying child, a son, Hans Christian Andersen. He himself never liked to be called Hans; to him his name was Christian Andersen; though abroad he is known as Hans, in the Anglo-Saxon world he is called simply Andersen, or H. C. Andersen.

His father was only a boy himself, twenty-two when his son was born. He was a shoemaker, but so full of dreams that he could not do well in everyday life; his shoemaking seems to have been poor. Once he made a pair of shoes as a sample for the lady of one of the great manor houses; he was hoping for the post of cobbler there, which would bring a country cottage, a cow, hens, a garden. A piece of silk was sent to him, but he had to provide the leather himself. All the hopes and talk of the little household were on those shoes; Hans Christian prayed for their success and when they were wrapped in a handkerchief and taken to the manor he waited expectantly for the good news; but his father came back pale and angry; the lady would not even try on the shoes and said he had wasted the silk. "Then I shall waste my leather too," he had said and had taken out his knife and cut the shoes to pieces.

Probably the elder Andersen felt he should not have been making shoes at all. Once Hans Christian saw tears in his eyes. It was when a boy from the Grammar School came in to be measured for a pair of boots and boasted about his books and all he was learning. Hans Christian saw his father turn away, his face quivering. "That is the way I should have gone!" he said.

These ambitions came from Hans Christian's grandmother. She was a blue-eyed well-figured old lady with fine ways that did not match her poverty and the rough neighborhood in which she lived. She felt that and, as she had a fluent tongue, she told endless stories about her aristocratic descent. It was not until he was grown up that Hans Christian knew that they were only stories, but from the very beginning he realized that there was a shadow over the family; his grandfather was a lunatic, harmless enough to go wandering about, which meant that everyone knew of him and saw him.

Perhaps this was why they made no friends, he and his father; his mother, Anne Marie, was always neighborly, but then she had not their pride. The young shoemaker was aloof; he gave all his love and time to his little son; sometimes it seemed as if there were not much difference in their ages. The father read aloud endlessly to Hans Christian from Holberg's plays and the *Arabian Nights*, and made him toys and a puppet theater. This ability to amuse children, to make enchanting things for them, was in the family; the grandfather carved queer wooden animals that he gave away to the children he met on his wanderings, and Hans Christian too, when he was older, made puppet theaters and he could cut paper into patterns with trees, flowers, angels, ballerinas, little men, umbrellas, and swans as fine as lace.

Every Sunday in summer Hans Christian's father would take him to the woods and lie dreaming and brooding on the grass while the little boy played. Once a year, in May, the mother would go too; it was her single pleasure trip of the year. She would put on her only good dress, a cotton gown in which she went to communion, and carry sandwiches and a pot of beer. In the evening, when it was time to go home, she would gather fresh beech boughs to plant behind the polished stove and St.-John's-wort to put in the chinks of the beams; they were an omen; if they lived, her family would live too, through the year.

They had only one room and a tiny kitchen—it can be seen today in the Munkemöllestraede—but she made it safe and comfortable and filled it with love. It is good to think that she had her reward; over and over again in his writings Hans Andersen went back to those days.

In his autobiography he wrote: "Our one little room had nearly all the space filled up with the shoemaker's bench, the bed, and the folding crib on which I slept. The walls were covered with pictures and over the workbench was a cupboard containing books and songs; the little kitchen had a row of shining pewter plates, and the small space seemed big and rich to me. The door itself with landscape paintings on the panels was as much to me then as a whole art gallery."

Those paintings are in the story of *Wee Willie Winkie, Ole Luköje,* who brings the children's dreams and squirts sweet milk in their eyes to make them sleepy.

Wee Willie Winkie touched the painting with his magic squirt, and the birds in it at once began to sing. The branches stirred in the trees, and the clouds scudded along; you could see their shadows drifting over the fields.

Willie Winkie took little Hjalmar and lifted him up to the picture-frame, and Hjalmar put his feet into the picture, right into the tall grass; there he stood with the sun shining down on him through the branches of the trees. He ran down to the water and got into a little boat that was lying there. It was painted red and white, and its sails shone like silver. . . .

Yes, it was a wonderful sail they went for. At one moment the woods were quite thick and dark, and then suddenly they were like a beautiful garden with flowers and sunshine, and there appeared great castles of glass and marble with princesses on the balconies who were all little girls that Hjalmar knew well and had played with. They reached out their hands, and each one was holding the nicest sugar-pig any sweet-shop could sell.

The small Hans Christian liked to be put to bed, not in his own crib, which was kept under the big bed until his parents were ready to sleep, but at the end of theirs. The wooden beds of Fyn are like four-posters set against the wall, and on them, for top bedclothes, is the Danish *Dyne*,[1] the feather quilt enclosed in a white linen case that serves as a top sheet and blankets. Probably the cupboard over the workbench was one of the painted ones of the island, roses and fruit on a blue ground, and the stove was of iron, chased in scrolls and giving out a tremendous heat. When the bed curtains were drawn they made a little house, but through them he could see the candlelight and firelight and hear his father reading, his mother's admiring or impatient interruptions, and he lay in a dream, half awake and half asleep, listening, letting the words sink into him while the simple room seemed the safest, happiest place on earth.

Anne Marie kept it all scoured and tidy and it was her pride to see that the sheets and muslin curtains were snow-white, and, as a practical background to the grandmother's fine manners, she taught her boy how to keep himself neat and clean in a simple economical way that was to serve him well. She dressed him carefully; his father's old suits were cut up for him, a handkerchief was tied round his neck in a bow, his head was washed with soap and his hair curled.

Anne Marie had too the genuine peasant feeling for life; she kept its times and festivals and, no matter how poor they were, on festival days she managed to serve the traditional food: rice porridge, a bit of roast goose,

---

[1] The Danish "y" is generally—not before two consonants —pronounced like the French "u" or German "ü."

and apple cake at Christmas, ham and green kale at Easter, and roast lamb at Whitsuntide.

Sometimes she used to look at Hans Christian and tell him how spoiled he was and how, as a child, she had been sent out to beg and was so ashamed that she spent the whole day under a bridge crying; though she was almost frozen she had not dared to go home without having earned a single penny. That must have gone deeply into the little boy's heart; years afterwards he made that poor child live forever in *The Little Match-Seller*.

So much that was in his childhood went into his fairy tales. From the kitchen off their room, a ladder led up into the attic, and in the gutter between the tiled roofs of their house and the one next door was his mother's only garden, a box filled with parsley and chives and herbs. In the story of *The Snow Queen* that garden still blooms.

> In the great city—where there are so many houses and people that there isn't room for everyone to have a little garden of his own, so most of them have to be content with flowers in flowerpots—there lived two poor children who *did* have a garden a bit larger than a flowerpot. . . . Their parents were next-door neighbors, living in attics; at the point where their roofs were almost touching and the gutter ran along the eaves, each house had a window . . . you had only to step across the gutter to cross from one window to the other.
>
> The parents of the two children each had a big wooden box outside and in this grew potherbs that they used and a little rose tree . . . they looked exactly like two banks of flowers. The sweetpea

tendrils hung down, the rose trees put out long branches . . . it was almost a triumphal arch of greenery and flowers.

Hans Andersen grew up with flowers. "I am the most Danish of writers," he was to say, and one of the most characteristic things in Denmark is the national love of flowers; perhaps only the Chinese and Japanese have surpassed it. In every house or apartment the windows are filled with plants, flowers and greenery, lovingly tended; they are almost a part of the family. "You can't trust the opinion of pot plants," says the butterfly in one of Andersen's Tales. "They converse too much with humans." All through the countryside are nursery gardens and hothouses, flower shops and flower markets where flowers are plentiful and cheap. It is a Chinese saying that a country where flowers are priced so as to make them a luxury has yet to learn the first principles of civilization.

Every Sunday, when the grandmother came, she brought flowers with her, and Hans Christian was allowed to arrange them in a vase to put on the cupboard shelf. It was always remarkable how his big hands could do delicate things with great beauty, cut that paper lace, dress puppets, make bouquets or garlands; almost the last thing we hear of him was of his decorating a chair with flowers for his hostess's silver wedding day; though he was an old man he would not let anybody help him.

The grandmother had charge of the garden of the lunatic asylum and sometimes Hans Christian was allowed to go there with her, especially when she burned the garden rubbish; but it was not only for the bonfire or the flowers that he went; with curiosity and terror he used to peep into the cells where the worst lunatics were kept. He was forbidden to go near them, but one day as he lay down looking through the crack under a door, he saw a lady, almost naked, lying on a straw bed; her hair hung down and she sang in a queer high voice that sent shivers down his back. All at once she sprang up and threw herself against the door; the little trap through which her food was put came open and she stretched out her arm; the tips of her fingers just touched Hans Christian, who lay screaming, paralyzed with fright; he was half dead with terror when the attendant came.

Perhaps it was this fright that made him dread and fear his grandfather. The old man was well known in Odense and the country round it; the housewives gave him food, the children liked him, but the boys sometimes chased him and threw stones. Once Hans Christian heard them; he hid himself, shaking with terror and pity, and felt sick with shame to know this was his grandfather, belonging to him.

Sometimes the boys teased him too; they jeered at his theater and his stories, and more and more he came to love his solitude. He stretched his mother's apron across a broomstick and the one gooseberry bush in the yard and sat there making up stories. In spite of the boys he liked to tell them—after all it is no good having stories that nobody hears—and sometimes he went to a room near the asylum where poor women came to spin; they petted him and, better still, they listened. He had picked up doctors' words like "heart" and "intestines" and "lungs" and he would draw fantastic pictures in chalk on the door to show how the human body was made. The old women said he was too clever to live, which pleased him enormously. He did not look strong; even then he was over-tall and thin, long-legged like a young stork, his favorite bird, which he was to resemble all his life; his skin was delicate from staying so much indoors, and his eyes were so small that they seemed to peer at people under his shock of fair hair, the flaxen hair of most Danish children. He had no idea that anyone thought he looked odd, and he drank in the old women's flattery as well as the even more horrid stories they told him of witches and ghosts, illnesses and cures, accidents and people who dropped down dead.

Anne Marie, too, was full of macabre peasant superstitions, all of which she faithfully did her best to plant in her son.

The great comet of 1811 showed in the sky when he was six years old. His mother told him it would knock the earth to bits or that at the very least something terrible was going to happen; Hans Christian stood shaking in his shoes as he looked at the frightful and mighty fireball with its large, shining tail until his father came out and quietly told him what it was, though Anne Marie did not believe it. To her, her husband was always saying appalling things; one day he closed the Bible and said: "Christ was only a man like us, but an extraordinary man." Anne Marie was terrified at his blasphemy,

Hans Christian expected the roof to fall, but nothing happened and the words stayed with him; he remembered other things his father said too: "The worst devil is in ourselves," and "I am a free-thinker." When he thought of them, they seemed to be pushing him on, in a way he did not altogether like, but no one can stay in his mother's house or under her apron always. The outside world, however big and frightening, has to be faced; one has even to learn to enjoy it.

One memorable day Hans Christian was taken to the theater. He gave no outward sign of what it was to mean to him; in fact, he was thoroughly unromantic. He stared more at the people than the stage and said longingly: "If only we had as many firkins of butter as there are people here, how I should eat!" but from that day the theater began to lure him; when there was no money to go inside, he would beg handbills and, sitting at home over them, imagine to himself whole plays round the titles and lists of characters. From the stories under the gooseberry bush he had progressed to drama.

Then his father decided that his son should go to school and Anne Marie took Hans Christian to the dame-school, stipulating that her boy was not to be touched with the rod.

The dame taught Hans Christian his letters and to "read right" as it was called, and to spell aloud in as high a key as possible. He liked it and there was a clock that he liked still more; little figures bobbed out when it struck the hours; he used to watch it and forget his spelling; the dame caned him and he took his book and went home.

He was sent next to a school for poor Jewish children. Even though the master was very kind to him he did not find happiness there. At the dame-school he had been beaten for the first time but here something happened that hurt far worse. He was clever at drawing and one day he showed a picture of a castle to a little girl; he wanted to impress her as he had impressed the old spinning women, as his grandmother had impressed, and he said it was a picture of his home and that, really, he was of high rank. When the child did not believe him, instead of stopping he tried to impress her more; he told her that God's angels talked to him. She drew away and said in a low voice to a boy near her: "He is mad like his grandfather." Hans Christian felt sick as he had felt when he heard the boys throwing the stones. Out in the world, people said things like that. He was frightened. It seemed as if the happy cosy home life was breaking up, and outside it everything was hard and chill.

It was the time of the Napoleonic wars. Napoleon was in everybody's mind and his picture hung even in the Andersens' little room. Hans Christian was always to remember how his father had revered the Emperor, and when, years afterwards, he visited Trianon and saw Napoleon's bedroom, he put his hand on the pillow for his father's sake. "If I had been alone I should have knelt down," he was to say.

Now the shoemaker began to talk and Anne Marie

to cry; she knew in her bones what would happen and knew too that her delicate uncertain husband was not fit to be a soldier; in a few days he had enlisted and soon Hans Christian heard him go away. He could not see the soldiers go because he was sick with measles in the big bed, but he heard the drums beating. Like other boys he had thought drums exciting, but now they were heartless and frightening; they were taking away his father. What was even more frightening was that he saw his grandmother break down. "It would be better if you could die now," she told him. He knew then he had been right to be afraid. His little world had fallen apart. At eight years old his childhood was over.

Like everything else the wars ended in frustration for the shoemaker. Before he reached them they were over. He came back, but the last spirit had gone out of him. He talked no more of ambitions and hopes and he was so thin that the bones of his face showed. There came a day when Anne Marie sent Hans Christian, not for the doctor, but for the wisewoman. The wisewoman was gruesome; she said incantations, tied a woolen thread round Hans Christian's wrist, and handed him a sprig of green that she said came from the tree that gave the wood for the crucifixion. "Is my father going to die?" he sobbed. She thought for a moment and made the comforting remark: "If he is, you will meet his ghost on your way home."

The poor little boy went home so distracted with terror that he could hardly walk. He met no one, but on the third day after that the suffering emaciated man died.

His corpse lay on the bed behind the calico curtains. Hans Christian and his mother shared the small bed and kept awake. A cricket chirped the whole night through.

"You needn't sing for him, he is dead," Anne Marie said to it. "The ice maiden has fetched him."

Hans Christian knew what she meant. In the winter before, when the windowpanes had been frozen, his father had made peepholes with hot pennies. Looking through them they thought they had seen a figure like a young girl with outstretched arms. "She has come to fetch me," his father had said and laughed.

Now he was dead, a young man with an old tired face. His last wish for his son might be said to have been an echo of his own wistful, wasted life. "No matter what the boy wants to be," he had told Anne Marie, "even if it were the silliest thing in the world, let him have his way. Let him have his way!"

II

WHILE his father lived Hans Christian had had someone
to whom he could look up. The elder Andersen, though
he was only a poor cobbler, had had wit and intellect,
he could assess and criticize his son, but now Hans Christian was quite uncurbed.

His mother said openly that he was the most remarkable boy on earth. She often told of a time when they
had gone gleaning in a place where the bailiff was well
known for being rude and savage, and as they picked up
the fallen corn they saw this man coming with a whip in
his hand. Anne Marie and the other women ran away,
but Hans Christian lost his wooden shoes and could not
run in the stubble. The bailiff came angrily up and had
lifted his whip when the small boy looked up at him and
said: "How dare you hit me when God can see it?" The
bailiff lowered his whip and asked Hans Christian's
name, patted him on the cheek and gave him money.

"Yes, my Hans Christian is a strange child," said his
mother proudly. "Everyone is kind to him."

He certainly looked strange. He wore a long coat and
wooden shoes, and a cap with a broken peak. He was so
gawky and awkward that people laughed at him, and his
habit of shutting his eyes when he thought made people
think he was blind. He was wildly talkative, but there
were few who understood that talk, and he was very
lonely. With his father's death he had lost his best com-

panion; his mother went out washing all day, standing up to her knees in the cold river water, beating the heavy linen with a wooden beater, and Hans Christian sat at home with his toy theater, made dolls' clothes, and read plays, a strange little solitary.

His mother sent him to school again, to the City School for Poor Boys, but only religion, reading, writing, and arithmetic were taught, and taught so badly that he did not really learn. The boys often persecuted him; he could not resist telling stories and one day the whole class chased him through the streets jeering: "There runs the playwright." It was his grandfather over again and it filled him with horror. Was he really like his grandfather as the little girl had said? After that he did all he could to avoid the other boys, and clung to his few real friends, all grown up.

Near the school was a house belonging to two ladies, the widow and sister of a pastor who had been a poet. Sent there one day on an errand, Hans Christian had seen in the house more books than he had ever imagined could be in one home; his wonder, and more particularly his reverence, attracted the attention of the two ladies and they invited him in. He was soon a regular visitor and a welcome one; he came as often as he could, to listen to their reading and borrow books, to talk and not be laughed at. In the Museum at Odense is a clumsy satin pincushion, once white, now soiled to a gray yellow; it is a pincushion that Hans Christian made for the pastor's widow, sewing it in gratitude and love.

In that home he heard Shakespeare for the first time

and soon he was acting Hamlet on his doll stage. Unlike most children he loved people to die in a play, it was dramatic, but it was not only the drama that stirred him; even in translation the poetry of *Hamlet* and *Lear* and *Midsummer Night's Dream* took hold of him. He was beginning to understand that it was something rare and great and splendid to be a poet. "My brother the poet," the spinster sister would say, her voice thrilling; fired, Hans Christian wrote a play of his own, a tragedy called *Abor and Elvira*.

He was never shy about reading his work and he read *Abor and Elvira* to everyone, without a doubt that they would admire it as much as he did; but a neighbor whose son was notoriously stupid made a joke, in Danish, *Abor* is very like the word for a fish, the perch, and she said: "You shouldn't have called it *Abor and Elvira*. You should have called it *Perch and Cod*." Cod! For his exquisite Elvira! It was one of the bumps of authorship and he took it badly. The whole play was spoiled for him forever, though his mother said wisely: "She only said it because *her* son couldn't have written it."

But if someone is a real, dyed-in-the-blood writer nothing can stop him, not even ridicule. Hans Christian began a new piece in which there was to be a king and a queen. He thought royal people should not speak like ordinary men and women but in some kind of a foreign language, which shows his perception, as German was spoken at the Danish court then; he borrowed a dictionary in which were English, French, and German words with Danish meanings and made up a language of his own. *"Guten morgen mon père, har de godt sleeping?"* his princesses asked their father. He was charmed with that.

Like all children he loved making lists, and he made a list, in his father's old army pay-book, of all the plays he meant one day to write; as the plays themselves were not written, he read the list aloud to anyone who had time to hear it. That dirty little pay-book is now one of the treasures of the Royal Library in Copenhagen.

He wrote poems too, but most of his time was spent in dreaming or reading. He could not spell or write a clear sentence or do the smallest sum, but he devoured any book he could get hold of and learned whole pieces of them and scenes of plays by heart. But this happy private life had to come to an end; Anne Marie said he must go out to work and she apprenticed him to a weaver.

His grandmother took him there the first day, and said bitterly that she had not expected to live to see the time when her grandson should mix with poor ragged boys and coarse men.

At first it was not as bad as she had made Hans Christian fear. The journeymen were not at all unkind to him; he was an original and amused them so that they protected him from the boys; when they found he had a gift for reciting and singing they would stop the looms and let him entertain them. It was as flattering as the old spinning women and it suited Hans Christian very well; he sang, and acted scenes from Shakespeare, Holberg, and his own plays, and he was happy until one day the journeymen said he must be a girl, his voice was so pure

and clear and high. They seized hold of him by his legs
and arms and began to investigate. Hans Christian tore
himself loose and fled home to his mother and refused
ever to go there again. She tried him in a tobacco fac-
tory but the jokes were the same and the tobacco dust
hurt his chest and made him cough; remembering his
delicate father she took him away.

She had been a widow for two years and she was a
full-blooded lively woman; before she had married Hans
Christian's father she had had an illegitimate little girl,
Karen Marie, who had been bundled out of the way into
a foster family. Now Anne Marie married again and
Hans Christian had to see everything his father had
loved go to another man; the new husband was a shoemaker too and he worked at the bench Andersen had
made, slept in his bed, called Anne Marie wife. It was
not only that. Hans Christian was supplanted himself;
he had to share his mother's attention with this stranger
who pushed him, not unkindly but firmly, out of the
way. The stepfather's family thought the marriage beneath them and would not allow either Anne Marie or
her son to come into their homes. It was very bitter that
he, Hans Christian, the wonder child, who could write
plays, who had elegant well-read friends, was not thought
fit to go into a workman's house! Proudly he said he did
not care. Why should he? He was going to be famous.
But he said it almost in a panic.

His mother was talking now of making him a tailor.
He was perpetually sewing dolls' clothes for his theater,
his hands seemed able to do anything. "Look at Master

Steegman," she urged him; "he has a shop in the main street, with big windows. He has journeymen. Look how rich he is!" But Hans Christian would not look. All at once he knew what he would be, an actor. "Actors are whipped, and have to live on oil to make them supple," said Anne Marie in horror. She was thinking of acrobats, but in any case Hans Christian was not listening. He was thinking of heroes. A hero went through unimaginable hardships but in the end someone, a patron or a nobleman or a fairy, helped him to fame; the fame always came, only you had to be a real hero.

The stepfather had moved the household to a new home where the garden ran down to the river. Hans Christian used to stand there away from the house on one of the big stones his mother used for washing, and sing, not only to himself. One of the old washerwomen had told him that China lay under the Odense River and he imagined how a Chinese Prince might hear him and be so enchanted with his voice that he would come up through the river to take him down to wealth and fame on the other side of the world, letting him come back again, of course, in the end to Odense, where he, Hans Christian, would build a great house like the Prince's palace in China; that palace came years after into the tale of *The Nightingale*.

The Emperor's palace was the finest palace in the world, made entirely of delicate porcelain. It was all so precious and fragile that you had to be tremendously careful how you touched anything. The garden was full of the rarest flowers, and the loveliest of these had little silver bells tied to them which tinkled so that no one should go by without noticing them. Yes, everything in the Emperor's garden was most carefully thought out, and it stretched so far that even the gardener had no idea where it ended. If you kept on walking you found yourself in a glorious wood with tall trees and deep lakes. The wood went right down to the sea, which was blue and deep; big ships could sail right in under the branches of the trees.

It was not only for the Prince that Hans Christian sang but for someone more practical. On the other side of the palings lay the big garden of one of the town's rich men and Hans Christian knew that this burgher sometimes brought his visitors to listen quietly behind the palings to him, the poor boy. He had a very pleasing voice and soon people began to send for him to come to their houses and sing. Among them was a handsome colonel of the dragoons, Colonel Höegh-Guldberg. The Guldbergs were perceptive learned people and the colonel noticed something in Hans Christian that struck him as more than just amusing and precocious; he decided the boy should have an audience with the Prince Governor, afterwards King Christian VIII.

This is not as dazzling as it sounds, because in Denmark the royal family is on friendly and easy terms with the people. Even today, in the throne room of Christiansborg Castle at Copenhagen, when he is in the capital, the King once a fortnight grants an audience to any of his subjects who have reason to ask for it.

For Hans Christian it was dazzling enough. Before

the interview, Colonel Guldberg told him, if the Prince
gave him an opportunity, to ask to be sent to the Grammar School. This dashed Hans Christian a little. He had
come to despise school; Anne Marie boasted so much
that her son could learn his lessons by taking one look
in his school books that soon he never looked at them at
all; he did not mean to waste this glittering opportunity
in talking about school, and standing before the Prince
in the long room at the Palace, he said firmly and fear-
lessly that he should like the Prince to help him to be an
actor and immediately began to recite. The Prince did
not smile nor clap; he only said sensibly that though
Hans Christian's reciting was good, that was no mark of
genius and he would far better apprentice himself to a
turner, as that was a respectable trade.

No one ever had more good advice than Hans Andersen. All his life long, people told him so many things
for his own good that it is a wonder he managed to exist at all. It was not that he did not feel criticism; he did,
inordinately, and he had a terrible way, that he could not
prevent, of bursting into tears though they shamed him
bitterly. He felt every word but there was a certainty in
him that was stronger than all the advice put together.

He managed not to cry at the Palace but to bow to
the Prince and get himself out of the room, but he was
deeply disappointed; what cut him to the heart, though,
was that he found all his friends, Colonel Guldberg, the
burghers at whose houses he had been to sing, even the
pastor's widow, thought he should do as the Prince said.
Some of them told him plainly why; a boy who was so

ludicrously lanky, they said, could never act and, even if he had been better looking, there was his background of poverty and, they said more gently, of insanity. It was clearly impossible and when Hans Christian would not give in they thought him tiresome and, one by one, they dropped him.

Anne Marie sometimes thought he went out of his way to make trouble for himself. There were two classes for confirmation every year in Odense, the dean's class and the chaplain's; a child was supposed to be allowed to choose either, but automatically the rich children, the children of quality, went to the dean, the poor to the chaplain, but when the time came for Hans Christian to be confirmed he chose to go to the dean.

"But why?" asked Anne Marie. "They will only look down on you. Why the dean?" Hans Christian could not exactly say why; if he felt he belonged, by right, to the gentler, educated children, he was also mortally afraid of being shut in with the rough, poor boys. He went to the dean but he paid for it. The dean himself was coldly distant with him and found fault with everything he did and said; the other children sneered and made him feel he had pushed himself in where he did not belong; only one little girl looked kindly at him and once she gave him a rose.

A poet is a poet, not only in his writing, but in feeling; a little is always enough for him because to him nothing is simply itself; it has a meaning, double or a thousandfold according to his vision; he is easily cluttered and it is a sign of the true poet that he would rather have one rose than a bouquet. To Hans Christian this was a very special gift, taking away the soreness, the unkind barbs, and he was quite satisfied.

The day of his confirmation arrived. Anne Marie and the grandmother came timidly to the great cathedral to hear their boy make his response. Hans Christian wore a brown suit of his father's, made over for him, a snowy white shirt, and, for the first time in his life, he had a pair of boots. His great fear was that everybody would not see them and he pulled them up outside his trousers. The boots creaked and that made him even more proud because he thought everyone in the congregation would hear and notice that they were new; then, with a pang, he realized that at this sacred moment he was thinking more about the boots than about God. He knew that was dreadful and he began to pray frantically, but found he was thinking of the boots again.

Those boots are in the story of *The Red Shoes,* in which little Karen, who wore them, is exactly as he was then.

Everybody stared at her feet and, as she walked up the aisle to the chancel, she felt that even the old pictures over the tombs, those portraits of the clergy and their wives in stiff ruffs and long black garments, were fastening their eyes on the red shoes. It was these that filled her thoughts when the priest laid his hand on her head and spoke of holy baptism, of the covenant with God and of her duty now to become a fully fledged Christian . . . and the organ played so solemnly and the children sang so beautifully . . . but Karen thought of nothing but her red shoes.

The traditional savings bank of Danish children is a clay pig; even nowadays they are sold in all the towns and villages, fat pigs in clay or china with a slit in their backs. Hans Christian's was an ordinary clay one but it held all the money he had saved in fourteen years, stray pennies he had been given, money from his singing or that he had earned by running errands. He had never touched it but, when his mother began to talk more urgently of tailoring, he saw that something desperate must be done; he must break his pig open, take his money, and go to Copenhagen.

When the pig-money was counted it was found to be thirteen rigsdaler. It was much less than as many American dollars of the time but to Hans Christian it was wealth and he begged his mother to let him go.

"But what will you do there?" she asked in bewilder-ment.

He gave his perpetual answer. "I shall be famous."

"But how? How?" asked Anne Marie.

Hans Christian knew all about it. "First you suffer terrible things," he said, "terrible things, but then you get to be famous."

He said "famous" so much as if it were the logical outcome that Anne Marie believed him but there was a general outcry when it became known that she had said "Yes." The neighbors said it was a dreadful thing to al-low so young a boy to go such a long way off and to a

big city where he knew no one. Anne Marie was shaken
but when she attempted to retract and say "No," Hans
Christian sobbed and cried. "Tell him to put it out of his
head," said the neighbors. He would not put it out of
his head and he reminded her of what his father had said:
"If it's the silliest thing in the world, let him do it."

Anne Marie herself was growing weary; her new husband was lazy and instead of having someone to work for
her she had to keep him as well as herself and Hans
Christian. All day she stood washing in the river; the
cold of the water was giving her rheumatism and she had
begun to take nips of brandy. It was the only thing, she
said, that kept out the cold but it cost money. Patheti-
cally, it was probable that this was the first time she had
wanted money for herself. She had done her best to start
Hans Christian properly in life and she knew she could
not afford to keep him idle at home. She did not really
believe he would reach Copenhagen. "He won't get any
further than Nyborg," she said to the neighbors. "When
he sees how rough the big sea is, he will come back."

Hans Christian made his plans. That summer some of
the actors and singers of the great Theater Royal had
come to Odense; they had filled his imagination, and he
had heard of the ballet, where a solo dancer, Madame
Schall, was the most popular. Now he had the idea of
going to one of his friends, Iversen the printer, and asking him for a letter of introduction to this Madame
Schall. "But I don't know her!" said Iversen. To Hans
Christian that did not matter in the least, and he went
on pleading for the letter. The old man earnestly ad-

vised him not to go to Copenhagen at all but to learn a trade. "That would be a great sin!" said Hans Christian.

Impressed in spite of himself, Iversen wrote to Madame Schall. "But she won't help you," he said and told Hans Christian to go and see a Professor Rahbek, a director of the Theater Royal. Hans Christian hardly heard, he was too pleased with the precious letter.

His mother packed his clothes in a small bundle. She had made a bargain with the driver of a post carriage who agreed to take Hans Christian to Copenhagen with him for three rigsdaler if the boy would join the coach outside Odense and get down on the outskirts of the capital so that he, the driver, could pocket the money himself.

One afternoon Anne Marie and Hans Christian went to the city gate. He wore his old shabby clothes; they thought his confirmation suit too smart for traveling and it was folded in the bundle, but he had on his boots and a hat so much too big for him that it fell down over his eyes. His little store of money was in his pocket, he carried his bundle in his hand, and he had a packet of bread rolls to eat on the way. He was just fourteen years old but far taller than his mother.

The old grandmother had walked out all the way to the gates to see him go. As the coach drew up, she sobbed without being able to say a word. Hans Christian never saw her again, she died in 1822, nor could he ever find her grave as she was buried in the burial ground for the poorest people, where the graves were not marked; he knew how she would have hated that.

He could not speak either. He kissed her and Anne Marie over and over again, then swung himself up and the guard blew the horn. It was a glorious afternoon; the sun, as much as tears, blinded his eyes as he looked back and saw the figures of his mother and grandmother, clinging together and growing smaller and smaller in the distance.

III

IT was from the hill of Frederiksberg, with its palace
and park, where the driver put him off, that Hans Christian first looked down on Copenhagen. In the fine September morning the city looked beautiful and promising
with its pale-green spires, its towers and buildings rising
out of the early mists. In those days the ramparts were
green round the city, and behind them a line of water
glinted in the sun, the water of Öresund separating Denmark from Sweden.

He had been terribly frightened. This compulsion
that is in some people, not coming from circumstances
outside them but dictated from within, making them
drive their flinching bodies on, overriding their natures, is
one of the strangest and most interesting things on earth;
Hans Christian did not know himself why he had not
turned back a dozen times. For two days and nights he
had traveled across the islands; when the coach had
stopped at the small towns on the way, Nyborg, Korsör,
Slagelse, Sorö, Roskilde, and the other passengers went
into the inns, he had had to stand outside, by a wheel,
eating the dry bread Anne Marie had given him; the
smell of good hot food reached him from the kitchens
but he had not dared to spend any of his money.

The ferry had been worst of all. Nowadays the ferry-
boats with their broad decks, white paint, the red band
round their funnels, cross the Great Belt in an hour and

a quarter, but in 1819 a small smack left at dusk and sailed all night. As Anne Marie had predicted, Hans Christian was terrified; he had stayed awake all night, thinking every moment they would go down to the bottom. When they reached Zealand, he felt so tired and forlorn that he knelt down on the dock behind a shed and asked God to help him.

Being Hans Christian, he had not, of course, traveled without making friends; there was a woman, a wet-nurse returning from Odense to Copenhagen, who was kind all the way and had insisted on giving him her address. Now, on this sparkling morning, he could not believe he would need it, and carelessly stuck it in his pocket as, his bundle in his hand, he walked marveling through the great park, along an avenue of linden trees, and finally found himself at the West Gate of Copenhagen.

In those days the city, being still walled, was guarded at the gates by soldiers and customs officers, who took a list of the passengers who came in by every coach. The King liked to see these lists and it seemed quite fitting to Hans Christian that the King should know of his arrival. It was part of this glorious day, the day he first trod the streets of Copenhagen. They were cobbled like those of Odense but were far wider and some of the houses were five or six stories high, which seemed immensely tall after the one or two stories at home. At first Hans Christian was so overawed that he could only wander about and stare, and it was some time before he remembered that he had to find food and shelter and

looked for an inn. He found one just inside the gate, arranged to leave his bundle there and come back that night
to a cheap garret room, and went out into the streets
again.

They seemed unaccountably swarming and noisy even
for a city. There were catcalls and screams, the smash of
broken glass; then soldiers on horseback came charging
through the crowd. He was in the middle of an anti-
Jewish riot.

Only one thing kept Hans Christian from running
back to the inn: his burning desire to find the Royal
Theater.

In Copenhagen, at that time, the Theater was the
center of all Danish cultural life and fashion; other, bigger countries should pause and think that as far back as
1819 Denmark had a national theater to which was attached its own company, its own singing school for opera, its own ballet and ballet school, all subsidized by
the State, and at which opera, ballet, and drama, both
classical and modern, were regularly produced; it gave an
impetus to the arts of the whole country; the best of her
writers, composers, painters, choreographers, actors, singers, and dancers were drawn there as to a magnet; but to
Hans Christian it was even more; he went there rather
as a pilgrim to a shrine and, when it was found, walked
round it, looking lovingly even at the walls, at its orna-
mented cornice and the two big pillared entrances, and
he prayed fervently that this would be the place where
God would let him be an actor.

A tout came up and asked him if he would like a

ticket. This seemed a generous gesture from the capital to its visitors and Hans Christian gratefully said yes. The tout told him the different kinds of seats and asked which he would like. "Whatever you are kind enough to give me," said Hans Christian naïvely and held out his hand.

"Be off, you great gawk!" said the man furiously and drove him away. After the happiness and ecstasy the rude words hurt; they seemed like a bad omen, and that was worrying because the next day was the one Hans Christian had set apart for the momentous call on Madame Schall.

In his little garret, he dressed himself carefully in his clean shirt, the confirmation suit, the high boots—this time put on under his trouser legs—and last of all, the hat that came down over his eyes; he said a prayer, took the letter Iversen had written, and set out to find the address.

It puzzled him as he had no experience of apartment houses but at last he went up a wide staircase and found the right door; before he pulled the bellrope, just to make sure, he knelt down and prayed again that she would help him.

Madame Schall, having been in the theater till midnight, got up very late and Hans Christian, in his eagerness, had come very early, so that he had to wait for what seemed hours on the landing. He sat on the cold stairs in a horrible tension of apprehension and hope; also growing exceedingly hungry.

When he was finally shown in, it was to the drawingroom where Madame Schall was resting on the sofa; he had not seen a lady do that in the daytime and he felt awkward towering above her. In the first quarter of the century, a fashionable room still had a Regency elegance and bareness; probably Madame Schall as a first dancer and favorite was well enough off to have the gilt chairs with spindle legs and satin seats, the console tables and mirrors of the period. It must all have looked disconcertingly fragile and glittering to the clumsy country boy, though he had seen the Prince Governor's Palace and the rooms of rich burghers in Odense, and he stood in front of this wonderful lady, trembling and blushing.

She was staring at him as if he were a monstrosity; she said she had never heard of Iversen; though Hans Christian knew she had not, it seemed a snub. Then she asked him some questions and he picked up his courage and began to tell her his hopes and schemes. Once he had started, it was easy, it all came tumbling out and he finished by telling her of how his plan of coming to Copenhagen to be an actor depended on her, and would she please help him.

She asked in a bewildered voice what parts he thought he could play. "Anything," said Hans Christian promptly. "I can show you. I shall play you a part from *Cinderella*. May I take off my boots?" he said seriously. "I am not light enough for the character with them on."

While she watched, helpless and a little frightened, he shook off his boots, stood them in a corner, and, taking off his hat, which he used as a tambourine, began to dance and sing; he had seen the play when the Royal Theater Players gave it at Odense and he thought it would compliment Madame Schall if he danced the heroine's part, which he did with wild uncouth gestures and great leaps that shook the room.

In Odense he had been the wonder child but, strangely, here there was no applause. Instead Madame Schall stopped him and told him sternly to get dressed at once and go away. Tears rolled down his cheeks as he put on his boots and Madame Schall saw them and seemed sorry. She told him more gently that sometimes he could come and eat a dinner at her house, a thing many Danish householders allowed poor students to do. Hans Christian wanted so much more than dinners that he turned away his head.

Outside he sat down on the stairs trying to think what to do. Old Mr. Iversen, he remembered, had seemed to know Madame Schall would not help him and had advised him to go and see Professor Rahbek at the Theater. Hope rose again as Hans Christian decided he had better do that.

It is ironic that Rahbek, who devoted his life to writing and literature, had no way of knowing that it was Hans Christian Andersen who walked into his office that day; all he saw was a gawky country boy on a wild-goose chase.

He told Hans Christian shortly that it was the Chief Director who decided on the parts and admitted the students, and it was too late that day for an interview. Then he, too, told him to go. The whole day was wasted, and another night's lodging had to be paid for! Hans Christian was dignified enough to hold back his tears in front of Rahbek, but alone in his garret at the inn he cried hopelessly.

In the morning his interview with the Chief Director was very short. The great man said coldly and decisively: "You are much too thin for the stage."

But this was a new day and Hans Christian had new courage, though perhaps it was the courage of desperation. He did not mean his answer to be impertinent though it was almost that. "If you will take me and give me a hundred-rigsdaler salary, I shall soon grow fat," he said.

The Chief Director was not used to being answered back. "You would be ridiculous on the stage," he said cuttingly and added what stung worse: "The Theater accepts only educated young persons."

Hans Christian would have liked to leave at once, his cheeks were burning, but he was desperate. He asked if he might join the Ballet. Like Madame Schall the Chief Director must have thought he was mad, and said even more coldly that the Ballet accepted pupils only in May and, in any case, it did not pay a salary until the training was over. Then the Director rang the bell and Hans Christian was shown out.

It was a frightened and miserable boy who found himself in the Square again. He took out his money and looked at it; of all the wealth in the clay pig there were only a few coins left. It seemed no one wanted to help him at all. His confidence was gone. He stood there alone, in the September wind, a terrified forlorn child.

Among the coins was the address of the kind nurse in the coach. He asked his way to her house and when she opened the door, threw himself into her arms, and with bitter tears told the whole story and asked her advice. "Take the first ship back to Odense," she said. "That is the only sensible thing to do." Everyone, it appeared, was sensible except Hans Christian. "I should rather die," he said and took a scolding for obstinacy.

He left her and wandered back to the Theater Square. Go back to Odense! His very bones knew he had spoken the truth and he would rather starve, here in the gutter, than do that. He could hear the jeers and laughter. "There runs the playwright! He is mad like his grand-father." He even felt the stones. He could not go back, but what was he to do?

What he did only someone with the spirit of a Hans Andersen could have done. He put apart the money for his inn bill, gathered the remaining coins in his hand and went into the Theater and bought a ticket for the play that night.

It was *Paul and Virginia*, and when the curtain went up, completely forgetting everything that had happened, he lived every moment of the story on the stage; when the lovers parted he burst into such violent crying that all the audience in the poor people's boxes turned to look at him. Some women tried to console him, saying it was only a play and nothing to trouble himself about; they gave him a sausage sandwich and other people too

began to share their food with him. Hans Christian, who
always told everyone everything, told them all about
himself and how he was weeping because he was a Paul
and the theater was his Virginia and he was separated
from it forever. They all thought it very touching and
stuffed him with fruit and cake. Soon he began to feel
surprisingly better.

He had had some food at last and he slept that night,
but when he paid his bill at the inn the next morning he
had only one rigsdaler left. He decided he must sink his
pride and find some work with a tradesman; perhaps to
be an apprentice in Copenhagen was different from
Odense. The nurse had given him a bed for the moment and she helped him to apprentice himself to a carpenter. An apprentice, in those days, had to be bound to
his master and for this Hans Christian had to send for his
baptismal register and a recommendation from Odense.
While this was coming the carpenter, who was pleasant
and fair, let him move to his house and begin work; but
the experience at the weaver's was still fresh in Hans
Christian's mind and when the other apprentices and
the journeymen began to make lewd jokes he knew he
could not stay; he might try but he would not succeed.
It would be better, he decided once again, to starve. For
a timid boy Hans Christian could be very resolute; he
apologized to the carpenter and left.

When he had left the weaver's, he had had his mother
to run to; now he was quite alone. He felt he could not
go back to the nurse; she was so robust and sensible that
she would think his reason stupid; he could not explain

how he shrank from things that other people thought funny, and he wandered aimlessly through the Copenhagen streets.

It is odd to think that he wandered destitute about the city of which he would become its most famous citizen. Perhaps he walked in the Amalienborg, where the four palaces make a circle in the Square, and sentinels in bright blue and white uniforms and bearskins stand on guard. It is here that the King lives and he, Hans Christian, was one day to stay. Perhaps he walked in the stately St. Anna Plads with its big white houses, in one of which he would have one of his many lodgings. The harbor lies at the foot of the street, and he could have walked down to look at the beautiful Christianshaven with its ships and quays; then past the customs houses to the Langelinie where, now aloof on a rock, the statue of his Little Mermaid looks out to sea. Visitors come from all over the world to see her, and there are often fresh flowers in her arms.

He must have wandered back towards the magnet of the Theater, and presently down the Nyhaven, where now the sailors' shops and eating houses are; tall houses line it on either side; three of them now have plaques let into the wall to show that Hans Andersen lived there; he was always restless and changed his lodgings often. Perhaps he walked round by the Fishmarket, where, in the very early morning, fishwives in their green serge skirts and white coif caps still sit selling fish and skinning eels. The eels wriggle horribly when their heads and skins are cut off, and perhaps he turned away, sickened, to the fragrance and color of the flower market in the little Höjbro Plads. There was the Stock Exchange with its dragon-twisted copper spire, and the sailors' church, Holmens Kirke. Behind them now are the buildings of the Royal Library, where his manuscripts are kept as treasures.

Perhaps he dreamed a little as he walked, but wandering is tiring, hungry work; his feet must have been sore; his bundle felt heavy; it would soon be evening, and he was chilled and friendless, homeless and hopeless.

It was then that he thought of his voice. Everybody had always praised his singing and he had heard that a man called Siboni, an Italian, was the Director of the Theater Music School. Perhaps Siboni would help him? He gathered up his courage for this new try, but he was shivering with nerves when he asked the way.

It was Hans Christian's lucky day. Siboni was giving a dinner party—in those days people dined at four or five o'clock—the composer Weyse was there, Baggesen the poet, and other celebrated men.

The housekeeper answered the door. She was busy and was just going to tell Hans Christian peremptorily to go away when he burst into speech and, as with Madame Schall and the nurse, poured out everything that had happened, of his wish now to be a singer, of how he had suffered and tried, of Madame Schall, the Chief Director, and the whole history of his life. The housekeeper forgot the dinner while she listened, and when at last she heard Siboni's impatient ringing, she told Hans Christian to stay where he was; then she whisked into the dining-room and repeated the whole story so well that Siboni had the boy brought in.

There was no more need to explain. His white face and shabby clothes made their own impression; the diners were silent from pity. Then Siboni told him to sing and Hans Christian lifted up his voice while they listened attentively, their wineglasses still, their eyes on him. He sang, he gave scenes from Holberg, recited poems with his old verve, and then suddenly remembering where he was and why, he burst into tears.

The men had dined well and they were perhaps easily touched but they were nearly all of them artists and there was a spark in the odd boy that they recognized. Siboni promised to take him as a pupil, Baggesen was quite sincere when he said: "One day something will come out of him"; it did not even seem odd when he added gravely to the shabby tear-stained overgrown child: "Don't get vain when the public applauds you."

That was always Hans Christian's danger; with appreciation his whole being expanded; when the housekeeper let him out that night, he was almost delirious with joy and hope. He begged her to tell him if Siboni meant what he had said, if really he, Hans Christian, could become a real singer and have a salary; he needed a salary, he explained, as he had only about seven pennies left. Kind and motherly, she stroked his hot cheeks and told him the best thing he could do was to go and see Professor Weyse in the morning.

She knew very well what had been done for the boy that night. When Hans Christian presented himself at the professor's lodgings he found that that kind man, who had once been a poor boy himself, had wisely worked on the diners' emotions to take up a collection. He had over seventy rigsdaler for Hans Christian and Siboni's firm promise that if he could learn enough German, the master would teach him and give him dinner every day at his house. "Get yourself a quiet decent lodging," said Weyse, "and every month I will give you ten rigsdaler."

On Madame Schall's stairs Hans Christian had wept. On the composer's he kissed his own hand and lifted it up in gratitude to God, who, he felt sure now, had watched over him. He was half mad with joy and relief but he was not surprised; in the end, the hero always was triumphant, and when he reached the nurse's house, to which he felt, now he was lucky, he could go back, he sat down to write his first letter to his mother.

IV

ANNE MARIE showed Hans Christian's letter to everyone she knew in Odense. "You see!" she said. "He
hasn't been there one week and his future is made!" But
the way to fame is like mountain-climbing; when one
peak is climbed, another higher comes into view and
before it can be reached one has to go down, down into
the valley.

Siboni was an inspired teacher and he was kind; sometimes he gave Hans Christian a little money. "Have fun
with it," said the handsome big Italian, and he let him
have the run of his house; but the winter was cold and
cruel. The boy had only one pair of boots and when
they wore out he was walking literally in ice and slush.
He caught a bad cold and his voice broke. Gently Siboni told him to face facts; he would never make a
singer; he should go back to Odense and learn a trade.

Odense. A trade. Everyone said that to him and they
were hateful words. He was still a hero, someone or
something must deliver him from them; he remembered
that Colonel Guldberg, who had been kind to him in
Odense and given him that interview with the Prince
Governor, had a brother in Copenhagen, and that he
was a professor and a poet. A poet! That seemed propitious and Hans Christian promptly wrote to Professor
Guldberg and was told to come and see him.

Although Hans Christian for many, many years was

poor in money, all his life he was rich in friends; it was as if he touched people with some sort of magic. The busy overworked Professor Guldberg offered coaching in German and Danish; it was clear from the letter that Hans Christian could not even write his own language. Hans Christian was grateful, but he thought little of lessons and he went to see Dahlén, a dancer who had a school that had connections with the Theater, and begged him for a place.

Dahlén began by being amused—Hans Christian showing his steps was like a ladder dancing—but he ended by being impressed. The children who came to him were brought by their teachers or mothers, who pushed and praised them into notice; this boy was quite alone and Dahlén saw that his face had the peaked old look of beggar children; the broken boots with paper in the soles, the tight old coat, told their own story; Hans Christian never mentioned hunger or money, but spoke only of the theater; that was his necessity, his end; he wanted to study dancing only as a means, and, touched by his honesty and passion, Dahlén let him in.

Hans Christian went triumphantly back to Professor Guldberg. Here was something to take away the taste of lessons.

He had already been warned that there was no salary for student dancers and, while he trained, he had to live. Guldberg got up a subscription for which Hans Christian wrote the appeal himself. It began prettily: "My need for a time compels me to lay my fate in the hands of noble friends of mankind since I feel most deeply attached to the art of acting and born only for the service of Thalia . . ." but it lapsed quickly into his own sincerity and practicability. "I hope I may stay in the Ballet until I become an actor. . . . I shall receive only shoes and stockings. I . . . ask for the gift of a little sum each month until I can support myself. I shall work hard to make the time as short as possible." And people responded. Professor Weyse contributed, which made Hans Christian happy as it showed that important men believed in him; but when Siboni's two maids came and offered part of their wages, Hans Christian felt not only happy but humbled; he was responsible to them all and had to work hard to repay such goodness.

While he worked with Siboni, Hans Christian had been living in an old crooked house, Holmensgade No. 8, in what was then a distinctly disreputable part of the city. Even to Hans Christian the street seemed strange; there were ladies and girls at every window and visitors at odd hours. At first some of the women, who were dressed and scented in a marvelous way, called out to him and made him blush but soon they grew used to seeing him and let him alone. One young girl in the landlady's house had visits from an old man who she said was her father; Hans Christian used politely to let him in. Years afterwards in a drawing-room in Copenhagen he was introduced to a rich old nobleman covered with orders and was surprised to recognize the same "father." One wonders if the "father" recognized him. Hans Christian had been sleeping in a disused larder off the kitchen. It was not much bigger than a cupboard, it had no window, only holes in the door for air, and was so small that when he was in it the only chair had to be kept on the bed.

When the landlady heard of the new riches—and probably Hans Christian ingenuously told her about them himself—she was avid to keep him. "I will give you board," she said; "who better?" Hans Christian stammered that he had hoped and dreamed of a better room, a real room. "It's true it is small," said the land-lady, "but I shall let you sit in the kitchen, and here you are safe," and she began to tell him such lurid things about the cheats of landladies that were to be found all over Copenhagen that soon she had frightened him so much that he was begging her to let him stay. She seized her opportunity and said that one thing was certain, she could not take him for less than twenty rigsdaler a month.

Professor Guldberg had fixed his limit. "You must not pay more," he had said. Hans Christian implored the landlady to take him for sixteen; that was the very most. She only said that unless she had twenty rigsdaler in advance, out he could go to be fleeced and robbed, and she left the room.

He could not keep back his sobs when he was left alone. A portrait of the landlady's husband hung over the sofa and, like a child, Hans Christian wetted his fingers in his tears and put them in the dead man's eyes, whispering that he begged him to feel them and soften his wife's heart. Perhaps it was this, or perhaps the woman had been thinking it over and realized, wisely, there was not that much money to be squeezed from the boy and she came back and said she would take sixteen rigsdaler.

It is sad to think that Hans Christian knelt down and kissed her hand and that for a long time he thought of her as a benefactor.

With all the low and dreadful people Hans Christian met, some of them the dregs of the city, with all the misery in which he lived, he kept a childlike faith, not only in life itself but in people. It was an intrinsic part of his gift and it protected him. He was like his own little Match-Seller, left outside in the dark frozen street, who struck her match and, in the spurt of the flame, saw another life, lit up, gracious, lovely, in the squalor of her own.

Ah, but a little match—that would be a comfort. If only she dared pull one out of the bunch, just one, strike it on the wall and warm her fingers! She pulled one out—ritch!—how it spurted and blazed! Such a clear warm flame, like a little candle, as she put her hand round it—yes, and what a curious light it was! The little girl fancied she was sitting in front of a big iron stove with shiny brass knobs and brass facings, with such a warm friendly fire burning . . . why, whatever was that? She was just stretching out her toes, so as to warm them too, when—out went the flame, and the stove vanished. There she sat with a little stub of burnt-out match in her hand.

She struck another one. It burned up so brightly, and where the gleam fell on the wall this became transparent like gauze. She could see right into the room, where the table was laid with a glittering white cloth and with delicate china; and there, steaming deliciously, was the roast goose stuffed with prunes and apples. Then, what was even finer, the goose jumped off the dish and waddled along the floor with the carving knife and fork in its back. Right up to the poor little girl it came . . . but then the match went out. . . .

It was his own warm glowing imagination that pro- tected Hans Christian and brought him unharmed to his glory, as it brought the sad little Match-Seller to hers. "She was trying to get warm," the people said when they saw the used-up matches, but he added: "No- body knew what lovely things she had seen and in what glory she had gone."

He had need of all his matches in the months that followed. His landlady entertained men in the very kitchen where she had told him he could sit. Often Hans Christian felt impelled to go to bed at six—it had to be bed as he could not sit on the chair. He did not mind; he had a candle, a tray of supper, a book; and he had made himself another doll theater for which, with pennies the landlady gave him for running her errands, he bought little dolls and dressed them in scraps of velvet and silk he begged from the milliners' shops.

He had no money for clothes and shoes; it was diffi- cult enough to make up the sixteen rigsdaler. Guldberg allowed him ten each month and Weyse helped with more, but still it was not quite enough. Hans Christian met again the little girl who, at the confirmation classes,

had given him the rose; he had heard she was in Copenhagen and went quite naturally to call on her; he knew
he looked odd going to a rich house in his grotesque
clothes but he was so anxious to see her again that he
felt she would not mind. The little girl was a young
lady now, Miss Tönder-Lund—it was always a mystery
to Hans Andersen how girls grew up so quickly—but
he had been right, she was glad to see him. She introduced him to her aunt and friends, who found him refreshing in the way he talked eagerly to them with no
hint of toadying or flattery. His fund of stories and poems
amused them and, one by one, they began to ask him
to their houses, so that Hans Christian was soon in one
of the most exclusive circles in Copenhagen; they gave
him little gifts to help him and Miss Tönder-Lund gave
him some of her pin money.

Hans Christian was always matter-of-fact about his
begging; he took what he needed and no more and,
though he knew all the sordid small bitternesses of
poverty, he never learned to be avaricious. "A poet
should not gorge," he wrote in after life, but added:
"And he should not starve!" That was exactly how he
tried to live and he was fond of telling the story of the
sick King whose illness could only be cured by bringing
him the shirt of the happiest man; when the happiest
man was found at last, it was also found that he had no
shirt.

From one person to another Hans Christian was
forced to go, holding out his hand. Hearing that the
University Librarian had been a farmer's boy in Fyn,

he found the courage to go and see him, and soon the Librarian was letting him take any book he liked, "as long as they are put back." Hans Christian's appetite for books was as strong as ever and now he found the novels of Sir Walter Scott and a new land, Scotland, seemed to become a part of him. In real life the world seemed slowly opening up for him too. Professor Guldberg knew how difficult dry steady study was for his pupil and persuaded an old actor to coach Hans Christian in drama. Hans Christian took the lessons very seriously; he was given comic parts to learn, but that did not suit him at all and he suggested that he should play Correggio in the tragedy about the great painter. "But a hero can't be long and thin!" the old actor protested. Though he was hurt, Hans Christian learned the part and recited it so well that his teacher was moved. "Feeling you certainly have," he said, "but you can never be an actor. What you will be, God knows." As an afterthought he added that Hans Christian ought to study Latin grammar.

Study. Lessons. Latin grammar. They seemed to be words that were said to him over and over again. The son of the nurse from Odense had learned Latin and Hans Christian consulted her. She shook her head. "Latin is a terribly expensive language," she said, but good Professor Guldberg managed to arrange even this.

Hans Christian enjoyed being able to say he was studying Latin, it sounded grand, but he found it hard and dry. He felt he would far rather act, even though his teacher said he would never be an actor.

Everyone unfortunately said the same thing. Copenhagen was then a little city and Hans Christian had already become known; people told one another about this oddity of a boy and, through Miss Tönder-Lund, he met a lady-in-waiting to the Crown Princess; invited to see her in her little sitting-room at the Palace, he met the Crown Princess, who came in to look at him; she made him sing and recite and, when he had finished, gave him ten rigsdaler and a bag of fruit and sweets; he dared not eat them all and carried half back to the rapacious landlady, who knew where he had been.

The Crown Princess and other friends suggested he appeal for a grant to the King, Frederik VI, who attended personally to every detail concerning the petitions of his subjects, even such a humble one as Hans Christian. The petition was written with help from all his friends, but the King asked the Directors of the Theater for a report; it was a bad one. Hans Christian Andersen, it said, had no talent whatever and a most unfortunate appearance; his singing, acting, and dancing were hopeless. The petition was dismissed.

But he got on to the stage. As a student of the Ballet school, one night he was told that all the figurantes were to be allowed to go on with the crowd, all of them, even he.

This was the first time he was really worried about his clothes; the confirmation coat held together but it was in holes, he could not straighten himself to his full height because his waistcoat was too short and left a gap between it and his trousers, while his hat still fell down over his eyes. To Hans Christian these were difficulties, but of course he could not let them prevent his going on the real stage, though he kept well to the back hoping to escape notice. Suddenly one of the singers, who was known as a wit, seized him by the hand and dragged him forward into the bright lights. "Allow me to present you to the Danish public," he cried. Hans Christian ran off the stage, knowing, as usual, that tears were running down his cheeks.

Then the good-hearted Dahlén gave him a tiny part in a ballet he had written; it was only as a troll in a group of trolls but at last he saw his name in print: "TROLL—ANDERSEN"! He carried the program of the ballet round with him and lay in bed and read his name by candlelight, his name in print! He seemed to know what it was like to be immortal and, indeed, that program is in the Museum at Odense and another, like it, on which he had scrawled remarks about the players— one of whom was afterwards Johanne Heiberg, Denmark's foremost actress—is in the University Library at Copenhagen.

Though he was in effect a charity child, though his life was extremely uncomfortable and his landlady bullied him, Hans Christian had moments in those days of great happiness, even of exhilaration. He was young, he was in Copenhagen, he felt he was on his way! Coming back from a visit to the Crown Princess at Frederiksberg, he walked through the park round the palace; it was two years since he had been into the open country, and the spring morning, the budding beech trees, the young green, and the streams filled him with exuberant joy. He began to sing and threw his arms round a tree and kissed it.

"Are you mad?" a rough voice asked. It was one of the King's grooms and Hans Christian was so startled that he ran away, but nothing could take away the ecstasy of that morning.

He liked to go to Dahlén's house, where nobody minded his shabby clothes and naïveté and where the children welcomed him. He would bring his doll theater and his cut-paper patterns that he always made for the littlest ones; his child friends kept these so carefully that many of them, too, are now in the Museum.

When Dahlén had regretfully to put him out of the Ballet school, he still held on to the Theater. His voice had, in part, recovered its richness, and he went to see the master of the singing school and succeeded in getting a place in the choir. Soon he had more than one part on the stage though they were not, even he could see, brilliantly successful. Once he was chosen to be a Brahmin; in pink tights, his hair bound into the Brahmin's one lock, he looked so emaciated that next time he went to see the Crown Princess she told him he had looked like a scalded cat.

His talent for making exalted friends always helped him. He had come to know the Rahbeks, who led the Danish literary world. Rahbek hardly spoke a word to him, but Mrs. Rahbek listened sympathetically to Hans Christian's verses and stories, which he had begun to write down and never tired of reading aloud. One day she gave him some flowers to take to a woman friend and said, gracefully: "It will please her to get a bouquet from a poet's hand."

Hans Christian felt as if he were on fire. It was the first time anyone had called him a poet. He could have kissed Mrs. Rahbek's hand. The tears that came as easily for exaltation as for grief brimmed in his eyes, but this time he was not ashamed of them; he had seen suddenly, with those words, what he must do: write his way to fame.

V

ONCE before Hans Christian had had a glimpse of his vocation; it was when the pastor's sister at Odense had spoken with such reverence of poets and he had been moved. Vocation is a strong word. "An artist is the same as anyone else," that is often said; but he is not, he is set as much apart by his gift as a religious by his vocation and he often has to suffer and be martyred for it. Now Hans Christian saw he had been vowed to this even when he sat under the apron by the gooseberry bush, when he collected his old playbills, wrote *Perch and Cod*. When he said "writing" he meant writing for the theater; that it could be for anything else had not occurred to him.

He was always precipitate and now he began to write with feverish haste, not plays for his doll theater but, he thought, for the real stage. He proudly brought one to read to Mrs. Rahbek.

"But you have put in whole passages from Ingemann and Oehlenschläger!" she protested, naming two of the best-known Danish poets.

"Yes, they are so beautiful," said Hans Christian complacently and went on reading.

Oehlenschläger was a writer of stirring epic poems and plays; Ingemann was at that period a wild romantic. Hans Christian's admiration was unbounded. He had attracted the attention of another eminent man, Örsted, the gentle brilliant scientist who was to become one of Andersen's best friends and the earliest to see what had been written when the Fairy Tales came out.

He had others, less well known but faithful friends; among them the Jurgensens, a watchmaker and his mother. Old Mrs. Jurgensen told him of Racine and Corneille and she praised his writing; she said he might one day become even better than Oehlenschläger.

Hans Christian was only sixteen; all this intoxicated him and he began to skip his lessons and gave himself up to poetry and the theater. Who would not rather be praised by admiring ladies in drawing-rooms and spend evenings in the theater than work in a little room at Latin grammar? As one of the chorus Hans Christian had a free seat in the pit and the temptation was irre-sistible; soon he was out every evening.

It was a strange, hectic, uncertain life he led in those days and he had to make desperate shifts to cover its discrepancies. He could hide the fact that some days he had almost nothing to eat but he could not hide his clothes. Once, on a hot summer day, he went, in a blue coat someone had given him, to see some friends. It was a good coat but much too big, especially across the chest; even when he buttoned it up to his chin there was still a great bag across the front; he filled it up with old theater programs, which made him look as if he had an enormous bosom, but naïvely he thought no one would notice. He went jauntily into the drawing-room but soon everyone was asking him what was the matter with his chest; why was it humped? Why didn't he open his coat on such a hot day?

He had always seemed odd because of his quaint mannerisms, but he now had to make extraordinary contortions to hide a sleeve that had split, or to cover up one cracked shoe with the other foot, or to pull down cuffs that had ridden far up his bony wrists.

He had a superstition that what he did on New Year's Day he would do the whole year round; probably it was one of Anne Marie's omens. The theater of course was closed that night, only a half-blind caretaker was on duty; Hans Christian stole past him and found his way down the corridors, up dusty steps, past stacked scenery, on to the stage. It was icy and as eerie as only an empty stage can be; he thought of ghosts, all the people who had been there, forgotten actors, and singers silent now, who had once had hearts beating like his; he thought they were watching him from the wings; he thought of dancers, stilled now, who were once as quick and lively as the girls and boys who had worked with him at Dahlén's, and as hopeful. His skin pricked with terror and a desolation filled him, but he had come to act and he took an attitude; not a single line could he remember and he fell on his knees and said the Lord's Prayer aloud. That seemed better, more propitious than acting, and he went out convinced that he would that year speak on the stage. Drama was what he ought to study. Never mind what people said, never mind the Latin grammar.

Then Professor Guldberg found out he was missing those precious lessons; the professor had suspected his pupil was not studying as he should, but he had not expected anything as ungrateful as this. He had gone out of his way to help Hans Christian, had taken time he should not really have spared to teach him, and, worst of all, on his behalf had badgered other people; the professor had had more belief in Hans Christian than anyone else, except perhaps Mrs. Jurgensen, and now he was disappointed and angry. With his usual tears and with promises Hans Christian begged to be forgiven, but, perhaps because he was so steeped in the theater, he was over-dramatic. "Don't act a comedy for me," said the angry professor. It was no comedy to Hans Christian, but the professor would not relent. "I still have thirty rigsdaler of your money left. You can come and get ten of those a month till they are finished. Then I have done with you," he said finally, and pushed Hans Christian out of the door and shut it.

Every night Hans Christian had asked God: "Will it be better with me soon?" but he did not seem to be walking in God's way; now by his own fault he had lost his dearest patron.

In three months the subscription funds were gone. The work in the chorus was meagerly paid and now for Hans Christian a time began of such privation as even he had not known. How he got through the winter of 1822 he never knew. At midday, when Mrs. Jurgensen thought he had gone to dinner with one of his friends, he would go out and sit on a bench in the park, perhaps eating a piece of bread he had saved, getting up now and then to stamp his frozen feet, sitting again almost at once because he was so weak; but though he often went without food all day, he tried to hide his pitiable condition and he still went on striving, yearning, and persisting. His fingers were so cold that he could hardly hold a pen but he managed to write a play: *The Robbers of Vissenberg*, based on a folk tale from home. Miss Tönder-Lund paid for it to be copied and, trembling with hope, he submitted it to the Directors of the Royal Theater.

It came back with a letter that showed these were wise and not unkind men:

June 16, 1822

To the author of the play:

Returning The Robbers of Vissenberg, *as completely unsuitable for the stage, the appointed censors wish the author to know, regarding his personal position, that with the total absence of elementary culture and all knowledge, which this play shows on every page, it would be impossible even to the highest talents to produce anything which might deserve to be presented to a cultured public. They would be most content if this hint might induce the young man to seek, and his friends and patrons to procure for him, the instruction without which the career he is so eager to adopt forever must and will be closed to him.*

Holstein. Rahbek. Olsen. Collin.

At first Hans Christian was too disappointed and wounded to take in the letter's meaning; then slowly

it linked with other things in his mind: Colonel Guldberg in Odense telling him to ask to be sent to school,
the Chief Director with his "only educated young persons are admitted to the Theater," Professor Guldberg
and his Danish lessons, the old actor and the Latin grammar. Hans Christian saw closing down on him this thing
that he had shirked for so long, which was beginning to
seem inevitable, "Study."

But how? By what means? *With* what means? As if
to put him deeper into despair, he was dismissed from
the chorus.

Hans Andersen was often asked how he found the
courage to go on as he did. He might have said because
he had no other choice. Again, like the Little Match-Seller with the matches, it was his only means of life. Now
out of his hunger and despair he wrote another tragedy:
Alfsol.

It was hastily written. How hastily can be seen by a
story that Captain Wulff, the naval officer who was an
eminent translator of Shakespeare, often told, of Hans
Christian appearing like an apparition in his doorway
and saying: "You have translated Shakespeare. I am so
fond of him. But I too have written a tragedy. Shall I
read it?" Without waiting for an answer he opened a
manuscript and started to read. Wulff was as much
amused as angry; he thought too that this writer of tragedies looked as if he were starving and asked him to
lunch, but the boy only shook his head impatiently and
went on reading.

At the end Wulff, interested, asked him to come

again. "I will, when I have written a new tragedy," said Hans Christian.

Wulff remarked that that would take some time. "I think that in a fortnight I shall have another one ready," said Hans Christian.

Alfsol showed something more clearly than his other writings; something that could only be called quality; it was ludicrously clumsy, impossible as a play, but it was alive and, as he read it aloud as usual to anyone who would listen, a few people were genuinely impressed.

Already one of Hans Christian's strangely kind friends had persuaded a newspaper to publish a short scene from *The Robbers of Vissenberg*, and when he saw himself in print as an author, it was even more heady than the theater program. He lay awake all night, reading the printed piece, staring at it, his heart beating, and soon he had the idea of collecting his works, and publishing them by subscription as *Youthful Attempts*. He decided to use William Christian Walter as a pen name, William for Shakespeare, Christian for himself, and Walter for Sir Walter Scott. It was not vanity, he explained. It was love; he loved Shakespeare and Scott and, naturally, he loved himself. Though the Crown Princess helped, the book had few subscribers and the printer lost money, but before Hans Christian knew of this he was far away.

Mrs. Jurgensen had interested a clergyman in *Alfsol* and he had offered to submit it to Rahbek with a personal note which would make sure it was read by him and the other Directors of the Theater. At the same time he told Hans Christian to go and see the most powerful of all the Directors, State Counselor Jonas Collin; so it was that Hans Christian furbished up his old clothes and went humbly to the house in the Bredgade that was, more than any other, to become a home to him.

It was an ample framework building with wooden balconies overlooking the front door and a courtyard where a big linden tree grew. Probably there were children about, boys and girls whose names Hans Christian was to know as if they were his own, Ingeborg, Edvard, Theodor, Gottlieb, and Louise.

Jonas Collin, in his portrait, looks a calm, solid man with a high forehead, a long straight nose, penetrating eyes, and a mouth that seems extraordinarily resolute and decisive, though it is not unkind. He did not seem amused as others had been by Hans Christian's clothes, the way that wrists and shins stuck out of coat and trousers, the stains and patches, but he listened in silence. His comments were dry and he hardly spoke of *Alfsol*. Other people had appreciated it so much that Hans Christian had expected at least a little praise; he was nettled and thought Collin seemed more like an enemy than a friend; he left feeling that at any rate there was no sympathy for him here; but a few days later he was called to see the Directors of the Theater. He was ushered into a room where all four Directors were sitting; he stood in front of them, waiting.

What he expected Hans Christian would not have liked to have said; but in his inmost heart he had thought it was possible, just possible, that *Alfsol* was to be given a production; people had praised it and why else had the Directors sent for him? Perhaps he was to be attached to the theater as some few favored playwrights were, but that was hardly likely. Perhaps on the strength of *Alfsol* he was to be commissioned to write a play; that would mean an advance of money. With dry lips, a beating heart, eyes bright with excitement—all the things that fitted the occasion—he waited as Rahbek began to speak.

Alfsol was given back to him at once. The play, Rahbek said gently, was, like *The Robbers*, impossible for the stage. Most biographers seem to credit Collin as the chief instigator of this meeting but the prime mover was the aloof cold Rahbek. After reading *Alfsol* he had written a letter to the other Directors:

Sept. 3, 1822

On Andersen's Alfsol, as a drama, the sentence is soon passed; it is a collection of words and tirades without dramatic action, without plan, without characters, full of all sorts of reminiscences, Ewald and Oehlenschläger, Icelandic and New German all mixed up, everyday phrases in everyday rhymes; in short, it is not suitable for the stage at all.

On the other hand, if it is taken into consideration that this play is a product of a person who is hardly able to write coherently, knows nothing of . . . grammar and, moreover, in his brains holds a rummage of good and bad in a hotchpotch, out of which he picks at random, and yet still a few glimpses are found in his works . . . one cannot help wishing that a test be made what this peculiar head might become by instruction. I don't know whether my more influential colleagues credit us with being able to procure him either immediate Royal or other public assistance for studies, or whether it would be better to do this . . . by public subscription, towards which I would be glad to contribute my mite. . . . But that something has to be done with him, I am convinced, and recommend my wish on that respect to the closer consideration and influential support of my colleagues.

Rahbek

Quivering with disappointment Hans Christian braced himself to hear what he knew was coming; he was about to be told, sternly, to stop this pestering, to go back to Odense and learn a trade; he steeled himself to hear it, but what was this that Rahbek was saying?

The play showed a little real promise, said Rahbek, such promise that if Hans Christian Andersen were prepared to be serious and study with his whole heart he might some day write something worthy of being acted on the Danish stage. The room was very still as those words were said; their grave import seemed to reach into Hans Christian and stir him as nothing had stirred him before and in that moment he had a glimpse of what it meant to write a play for a great theater, of what it could mean to be a writer. The pastor's sister had touched him, Mrs. Rahbek's words had gone deep, but this was more. It was not an inflated dream such as he had dreamed for himself; it was reality; he quivered with a new feeling of humbleness; and tears, not his usual gush of easy tears but slow earnest tears, came into his eyes.

Collin looked at the boy's face thoughtfully but Rahbek went briskly on. The Directors had decided, he said, to provide for Hans Christian's education, State Counselor Collin would speak to the King; in fact, they had decided to send him to school.

School! After the great vision it was like a slap in the face. Hans Christian stared at Rahbek, dumb with astonishment. School! But he was a playwright and grownup; he was seventeen, the age boys leave school! For a moment he thought they were mocking him, but their faces were perfectly serious and gentle as they waited for him to speak.

Poor Hans Christian could not speak because he did not know what to say. He had lately come to know he must study, yes, certainly, but he had imagined it being in a dignified room full of books, tutored by a professor perhaps, working romantically far into the night—but school! School meant children, slates, exercise books, classrooms. He turned red and the whole of him felt offended; all of him, his tall body, the promise in *Alfsol* of which they spoke, his experience—after all, he had been in the chorus and the ballet, and for almost three years lived on his own in this big city, been made free of the Theater, welcomed and asked to read his verses in the drawing-rooms of Copenhagen. Then he saw, in a flash of insight, that all that was beside the point; what were important were those heartburning phrases that came back to him now, phrases that had burned themselves into him for always: "the theater accepts only educated young persons," "with the lack of elementary culture and education it would be impossible for the greatest talent in the world to produce. . . ." He saw now that they had been just. It was not unkindness, it was truth, and he looked with a new gratitude at the Directors.

These eminent men were serious over his gift, concerned; what was more, they were donating money for it and he, Hans Christian, more than anyone else, knew what a precious thing was money; and what were they asking of him? Very much. He would have to shed his hopes, all he had gained, his little acquired privileges, his conceits, everything, and go back to the beginning again. Half dazed, he managed to open his lips and accept.

He was told to go and see Collin in a few days. They all shook hands with him and a moment later he was outside in the Square, where more than three years ago he had come stumbling out after a rebuff from this same Rahbek, whose hand he had just shaken.

Where, Hans Christian might very well wonder, was life taking him now?

VI

IN the days that followed, an extraordinary feeling of peace and relief came to Hans Christian; it had been only too ordinary for him to live with worry and uncertainty and strain; now, slowly, he began to understand that he would, for some years at any rate, have enough to eat while he worked, that he would be given books, clothes that fitted him, shoes that kept water out, even that strange thing he had heard about but never had, except those long-ago gifts from Siboni, pocket money. All this Collin made plain to him. The King had been pleased to grant him an allowance from the public funds; every quarter Collin would send him money for his keep, clothes, books, laundry, and a little for himself and he would get free instruction at the Grammar School at Slagelse. "Slagelse!" said Hans Christian and his face fell, but the Counselor was so kind that it seemed ungrateful to be disappointed. Collin took Hans Christian home to dinner where Mrs. Collin gave him a real welcome.

The Collin children let few people into their circle; they had family jokes, family words, almost a family language, but their father said this strange boy, whom he had in a way adopted, was to be one of them and they took him in, making no fuss of him but treating him casually, not warmly, because it was their way even with each other to be cool, but really like a brother.

There was nothing here to frighten anybody. Though Jonas Collin was a powerful statesman in Denmark, he lived simply and the unpretentious house, the way he and everybody helped in the family, made Hans Christian breathe as easily as he had once, long ago, at home. It was all very different from the lavish and romantic drawing-rooms he had yearned after, but there was something he instinctively recognized as better; it was direct and simple, and, yes, high-souled, and in Collin he felt he had found another father. "Don't be afraid to write to me," said Collin. "Tell me anything you need and how you get on."

It was a heartened and hopeful Hans Christian who left Copenhagen by the stagecoach for school.

When he arrived at Slagelse he asked the landlady if there was anything remarkable to see in the town. "Yes," she said, "the new fire engine and Pastor Bastholm's library."

The sleepy little backwater was smaller than Odense; even its main street was cobbled and winding and its few red roofs, its copper towers, were set in rolling green fields and muddy lanes; it seemed very dull to the boy who had led the life, however poor, of a man about town and he badly missed the beauty and excitement of Copenhagen.

All the same, at first Slagelse promised well for him. His landlady cosseted him; his room was clean and fresh, he looked from the window onto a garden and fields; after the dark holes in which he had lived at Copenhagen it was delicious, and at the school itself the teachers seemed encouraging, but soon he began to see what he had undertaken by coming. "First you suffer terrible things," he had told his mother. "Then you get to be famous." Fortunately the terrible things had unfolded themselves one by one, and from the erossing of the Great Belt to the last penniless days in Copenhagen he had been able to endure them all, always hoping it would be better with him soon; now, when materially it was much better, he was tormented even more and in quite another way.

He had persuaded himself that it might be romantic to go to school and had written triumphantly to his mother and wished his father and grandmother were alive to hear this news which would have pleased them more than anything else. At one time his hopes had soared ridiculously, even to admittance at Sorö Academy, the Danish Eton. Soon he began to see there was nothing even remotely romantic about Slagelse Grammar School. It was humdrum and everyday; he was not used to sitting on a bench or working steadily or doing what he was told, but it quickly became too painful to be boring.

There was one thing that Hans Christian and perhaps the Royal Theater Directors had not thought of, and that was, as he knew almost nothing, he would have to be placed in the second lowest class among the little boys. Anyone who remembers anything of his own school days will know what an agony that was.

The little boys hardly reached to his elbow and here he was, stumbling and stammering over easy words and sums that they, in their quick brightness, could solve in a twinkling. He was taller than ever, too big for the benches and tables, and his awkwardness, his big head with its thatch of hair, the little eyes blinking behind the big nose, made him a perfect target for teasing. Yet they did not tease him as much as they might have done; there was something about him that made them desist— perhaps it was his palpable goodness and earnestness. Children can recognize those qualities, and Hans Christian never suffered as much from the boys as soon he began to do from the teachers.

After the first few weeks they found him, quite simply, exasperating. Overworked and very badly paid, they had a feeling of resentment against this youth who was financed by a State grant, nor could they see at all why he had it; to them he had nothing to distinguish him but size and ignorance.

"I had a great desire to learn," he wrote, "but for the moment I floundered about as if I had been thrown into the sea; one wave followed another; grammar, geography, mathematics." Hans Christian studied long after school hours were over; when he was stupid with sleep, he would wash his head with cold water or run about the little school garden to wake himself up. He worked desperately, fervently, and at the end of the first term his marks were not too bad.

Timidly he sent them to Professor Guldberg, telling him what had been done. Hans Christian had never ceased to worry over the breach with his old friend, and now he begged the professor to forgive him. He sent his

marks, he said, to show he was really working now, and
Guldberg wrote back a letter full of kindliness. "But as
your friend," the professor added, "I tell you, don't
write verses. Study."

That prohibition was echoed by the rector, but not
as gently.

The rector of Slagelse was Simon Meisling, a thick-
set, heavy, dirty little man with red hair and a fat choleric
face. He had the brain of a scholar and the tastes of a
bull. Hans Christian the day he arrived had innocently
gone to call on him and his big, rather blowzy wife; as
usual, he had told them his hopes, his secret schemes,
and read them poems and scenes from his plays. He very
soon learned how silly he had been. Easy Mrs. Meisling
had been impressed with him and soon became embar-
rassingly kind, but the rector who had looked at him
with cold eyes as he read, began to make sarcastic gibes.

The whole school was afraid of Meisling, and now
Hans Christian became his butt. "Shakespeare with the
vampire eyes!" he would call him, and if a herd of cattle passed, he would tell the boys to stand up and look
at their brothers; if, in spite of struggles, the fatal tears
came, Meisling would send a boy to fetch a brick so that
the great poet Andersen could wipe his eyes on it and
make even a brick poetical. It sounds a stupid brutish
humor, but thundered in front of a room full of boys, it
was oddly humiliating and Hans Christian's whole body
flinched and trembled as if it were being flayed; and the
silly tears flowed down.

He could not account for the rector's dislike; Meisling

had accepted him knowing what his ignorance was; sometimes, too, he was bewilderingly kind and asked Hans Christian to his house on Sundays and spoke so well of him that Hans Christian was happy; then suddenly he was angry. Why was he so angry? Hans Christian could not think why; it would be safe to say that never in his life had he felt jealousy.

Meisling was jealous; he had cause; coming from Copenhagen, sponsored by the Directors of the Theater Royal, Hans Christian was asked to homes such as that of Ingemann, the poet, who was teaching now at Sorö, not far away.

The Ingemanns were a refuge. Even the house in its willows, its lawn sloping down to the lake, was like poetry; "flowers and vines twined round the windows, the rooms were hung with portraits of distinguished poets. We sailed on the lake with an æolian harp made fast on the mast." Mrs. Ingemann, with her black ringlets, her big forehead, and eyes set in a small face on a delicate little neck, had the look, the quiet happiness, of a bird; and her husband, though he was already known throughout Denmark, was so charming and modest that he treated this overbig schoolboy as a serious fellow poet. "I really loved these people," Hans Andersen wrote of them. "There are people in whose society one is made better . . . that which is dark passes away and the whole world appears in sunlight."

Meisling would himself have liked to know Ingemann. There were also other people that Mrs. Meisling would dearly have liked to know, but she had made herself so notorious in Slagelse that there were few houses in the town to which she was asked; now she saw this charity boy invited and welcomed. She complained to her husband, and Hans Christian was stopped; if he went to those houses, said Meisling, he would be expelled, but the rector did not dare stop him from going to Ingemann's. Worst of all, when at the end of the first year they all went to Copenhagen for the Christmas holidays, Meisling saw his pupil disappear into houses like Collin's, Rahbek's, Captain Wulff's—men whom the shabby burdened schoolmaster would never know.

Hans Christian had no idea of this; to him the rector was nearly as powerful as God. He quaked when Meisling came into the class, and when it was Hans Christian's turn to recite to him, the little boys felt the whole bench shake; no matter how well he knew the lesson, and he always did know it, he could never say it in front of Meisling, who would then bellow at him and say he was a hopeless fool. Hans Christian was to have plenty of scolding in his life, but none as cruel as this; he grew so nervous that he thought he would be expelled when once, instead of the "remarkably good" he earned each week for conduct, the master in charge wrote only "very good." On that visit to Copenhagen Hans Christian had hardly dared to take his marks to Collin. "They will think I am wasting the money," he had thought in misery. To his amazement, Collin was pleased. "You have shown industry and courage," he said and asked Hans Christian to dinner at his house, where once again the boy met the Collin children. The eldest, Ingeborg, was really friendly, Edvard gave him a book, and Collin lent him the money for a new coat.

Yes, there were gleams of happiness in spite of school. This Christmas visit to the capital was, of course, entirely happy, and then he had a tiny inheritance from his grandmother's estate, though estate was a large word for it. When the taxes were paid, it was only twenty rigsdaler, but Hans Christian knew the munificent feeling of sending money to his mother and of paying Collin back for the coat, both of which things he did and pleased the Counselor very much. Hans Christian bought a little store of linen and books, the first, except for Edvard's gift, he had had of his own, and in the spring the Crown Princess, who did not forget him, sent him the money for a visit to Odense.

Coming back to those well-known streets, the one-storied timbered houses, the neighbors who struck him as unbelievably ragged and poor, he was able to measure how much he had accomplished since the day four years ago when he had met the coach outside the city gate. Though not quite as he had dreamed he would come back—from the Chinese Prince for instance—he was well dressed, with money in his pocket. His own mother, meeting him in the street, did not know him; when the tall stranger spoke to her she wanted to curtsy.

It was all happily successful. He stayed with Iversen, the old printer; he dined often with Colonel Guldberg and, wherever he was, his mother kept fetching him out to be shown to somebody else. Now they were saying that the shoemaker's son was not as mad as he seemed;

windows were opened for a peep at him; people pointed
him out, boasting they had known him as a child. Anne
Marie said he was being honored as if he were the child
of a count.

But the little triumph made the humiliations of school,
when he went back after the Easter recess, all the sharper.
The chief use Meisling seemed to find for him now was
as a nursemaid for his children. Hans Andersen was
never indiscriminately fond of children; no one is who is
capable of deep sympathy with an individual child, and
the little Meislings could not have been attractive. He
must have wondered if this was what he was sent to
Slagelse to do, separating noisy little quarrelers, amusing
the older boys and girls, carrying the baby, rocking it to
sleep. With his good nature he did it all, but it is to be
hoped he did not make any of his exquisite cut-paper
figures for these little cattle or tell them his stories,
though it is only too likely that he did. He would have
done anything to appease the rector.

How much this man preyed on his mind is shown by
reading his diary: "The rector said 'Good night' to me;
oh, if only he knew how his friendliness encourages
me. . . . The rector's frock coat was covered with
fluff; he called to the servant girl for a brush, she did not
come at once so I ran out and brushed him. . . . I
dread tomorrow's Greek. . . . God! My heart feels
as if it would burst. Got *bad* for Greek. What will become of me?"

The despairing writing goes on. He could not even
please the teachers; they had a pattern boy in their

minds and anyone who did not fit it was wrong; they
nagged and humiliated Hans Christian. Years afterwards
in *The Ugly Duckling* he wrote a scene that might belong to those teachers; it is where the duckling is in-
structed by a hen and a cat.

They always used to say "We and the world"
because they fancied that they made up half the
world—what's more, much the superior half of it.
The duckling thought there might be two opinions
about that, but the hen wouldn't hear of it.

"Can you lay eggs?" she asked.

"No."

"Well, then, hold your tongue, will you!"

And the cat asked: "Can you arch your back or
purr or give out sparks?"

"No."

"Well, then, your opinion's not wanted, when
sensible people are talking."

And the duckling sat in the corner, quite out of
spirits. Then suddenly he remembered the fresh air
and the sunshine, and he got such a curious longing to swim in the water that—he couldn't help it
—he had to tell the hen.

"What's the matter with you?" she asked. "You
haven't anything to do—that's why you get these
fancies. They'd soon go if only you'd lay eggs or
else purr."

"But it's so lovely to swim in the water," said
the duckling; "so lovely to duck your head in it and
dive down to the bottom."

"Most enjoyable, I'm sure," said the hen. "You
must have gone crazy. Ask the cat about it—I've
never met anyone as clever as he is—ask him if
he's fond of swimming or diving! I say nothing for
myself. Ask our old mistress, the wisest woman in

the world! Do you suppose that she's keen on
swimming and diving?"

"You don't understand me," said the duckling.

"Well, if we don't understand you, I should like
to know who would. Surely you'll never try and
make out you are wiser than the cat and the mistress—not to mention myself. . . . You may take
my word for it—if I say unpleasant things to you,
it's all for your good; that's just how you can tell
which are your real friends. Only see that you lay
eggs and learn how to purr and give out sparks!"

"I think I'll go out into the wide world," said
the duckling.

But Hans Christian could not go out into the wide
world. He had to stay there, on his bench in the class-
room at Slagelse. No one understood his longing and his
need for poetry.

Examination time was coming and he was full of
dread; he gave himself headaches and put himself into
cold sweats, but he did well, was put up to the third
class, and Meisling wrote a surprisingly good report to
Collin. The Crown Princess sent money again and, in
his second Christmas holidays, Hans Christian was able
to pay another longed-for visit to Copenhagen, though
Meisling, who longed to stop him, said he could only be
spared for a week.

When Hans Christian was happy he soared to dangerous heights, dangerous because in his happiness he
boasted and showed all his naïveté. Now he talked
loudly of all he meant to do and wondered aloud if he
should take Holberg, Shakespeare, or Walter Scott as
his model. Mrs. Wulff, always sensible, tried to bring

him down to earth, but earth did not exist for Hans Christian those holidays; he was up among the stars. He was away from the rector for a whole eight days, he was often at the Collins' house, the Rahbeks', the Wulffs', he read and dreamed poetry and went to his beloved theater. Sooner than miss the performance the last Saturday, he let the mail coach go without him and walked all through the night and the next day to Slagelse to be in time to play with the rector's children as appointed on Monday morning.

In 1824 and early 1825, two things happened that woke the young Hans Christian—he was now nearly twenty—to an even greater sensitivity than he had had before; it became so sharp it was often torment. In those days, Denmark still had capital punishment, and it was thought edifying that people, especially children, should see the executions. Near Slagelse a seventeen-year-old girl, whose father had objected to the young man she wished to marry, had incited her sweetheart and a farm servant to murder the father; all three were to have their heads cut off and Meisling ordered the older pupils to go and see it.

The execution was at dawn; the three were bound in a cart, the girl held in her lover's arms, leaning her head against his heart; she was deadly pale and her eyes seemed to Hans Christian to stare at him; behind them sat the laborer, livid with fear as his friends called out "Good-by" to him; he squinted and nodded in a ghastly antic of bravery. All three were made to stand by their coffins while a hymn was sung, the girl's voice rising hysterically above the rest. These moments were more horrible than the very moment of death, when, the girl first, one after another, they put their heads on the block; her sweetheart, coming next, had to put his face in her blood. There was an idea, Hans Christian had heard of it, that warm human blood was a cure for many illnesses and a poor epileptic was brought up and given a cup of blood to drink; he ran away in a fit. The men's heads were put up on poles, a ballad-maker went round selling verses which were put, as in *Frankie and Johnnie,* into the criminals' mouths, and fried eels and beer were sold as if it were a holiday.

Shuddering and shocked and sickened by everybody round him, Hans Christian managed to get back to the school, wondering why he was so different from other people; he despised himself, but all day and all night, and for years, he saw those white faces and the girl's eyes, and he heard her voice.

Then as the new year opened, the rector told him to come and live in his house. Mrs. Meisling had found out how useful he was, and why, she asked her husband, should a landlady have that two hundred rigsdaler? She had another reason. Hans Christian was a young man now, in the fourth class, which he had reached at last after passing the examination in fresh sweats of fear. He was still, of course, far behind the others, working with boys of sixteen, but he was catching up, growing mature; all the same, he dared not tell the rector he would rather stay in his quiet lodging and he did not know why, when Mrs. Meisling looked at him, his body felt hot and uncomfortable.

VII

MRS. MEISLING had always teased Hans Christian. Sometimes on Sundays the rector would play with his children and a few chosen pupils; it was boisterous, noisy, rough, and often questionable fun. He would insist on wheeling Hans Christian about in the perambulator and, as a forfeit, he would make Hans Christian kiss Mrs. Meisling under a blanket. Mrs. Meisling kissed thoroughly while Hans Christian flinched and blushed.

In the lax noisy Meisling house he seemed to live in an atmosphere of women, of swishing skirts, giggles, of intimate garments hung over chairs, of confidences. The maids knew what their mistress did and they behaved as they liked; they, too, thought it was fun to embarrass Hans Christian and they would come into his room, lean on his chair, interrupt him, and talk to him until Mrs. Meisling came and drove them away and took their place.

He had been given a room with a separate entrance to the courtyard, but now he found it had another door communicating with her bedroom and, with blushing cheeks and a beating heart, he would listen, dreading that she would come in. That he knew very well what she wanted is shown in his novel *The Improvisatore*, in which she is Santa, the buxom wife who tempts young Antonio, the hero. "You are handsome, you are good, my husband loves you, I love you," says Santa, and with these words Antonio felt a burning kiss on his brow, her arm clasped his neck, her cheek touched him.

"His blood became like a flame, a trembling went through his limbs, it was as if his breath stood still." In his room Hans Christian must have thought of just such highly colored scenes, but she was the rector's wife, a lady! At that he blushed more than ever. In the novel, when the husband comes in, Santa quickly says Antonio is ill. "I thought he would have fainted in my arms," she says brazenly as if nothing had happened. Antonio feels shame and indignation in his very soul, just like Hans Christian.

Mrs. Meisling's behavior was probably the reason for her husband's savage temper and heavy drinking; he had a great deal to bear; after he was asleep, she would put on a peasant dress and go out into the streets or woods to see what and whom she could find. Everyone in Slagelse knew of it. Hans Christian tried to keep his respect for her but he could not. Every time she came near him he tingled. He was thankful when he could escape to Copenhagen for Christmas.

He had been asked to stay at the Wulffs'. "Do they know you are a charity boy?" sneered Meisling. Hans Christian answered gently that they did. "Wonderful!" said the rector.

It was almost too wonderful. Captain Wulff was in charge of the Naval Academy, which was then in one of the pale palaces of the Amalienborg, and Hans Christian, shown to his room by a footman, looked down to where sentries stamped in the snow in front of the King's Palace. "Six years ago," he thought, "I wandered in that Square and no one knew me. Now I am staying in a house, next the King!"

The blessedness of space and cleanliness, quiet and dignity fell on his raw nerves. Collin once again was pleased with his marks. Ingeborg joked with him; he was often with Edvard and he read a new poem to Henriette, Wulff's daughter, and to everyone else and it was liked; Oehlenschläger smiled on him. Hans Christian began to believe that he himself was a little like Byron and resolved to fall in love with Oehlenschläger's daughter Lotte—all the fourth class had been in love— then, in the midst of this excitement, he had a letter from the rector, who said he had heard Hans Christian was making himself ridiculous reading his poems and he would have a few things to say when he saw him again! Hans Christian went back sick with fright.

The rector was posted to Helsingör and, like a pigeon on a chalk line, Hans Christian went with him; it seemed sensible; the students' examination at the University, equivalent to taking a degree, was to come in the next half year and the rector promised him coaching in Latin and Greek.

With the new place, the Meislings put on a new self-respect; the rector wore a frock coat, which he kept clean, and he refrained from bullying either teachers or boys; even Hans Christian had a respite. The ladies of Helsingör delighted Mrs. Meisling by calling on her but

the neighborliness did not last; whispers quickly reached
Helsingör and soon she was cut in the street and no invitations came; she relapsed into her old ways, and things
were even more miserable in this beautiful little town
than they had been in Slagelse.

Helsingör was romantic as well as beautiful; Sweden
could be seen across the Sound, the houses standing out
quite clearly on the opposite shore; the water was blue
and calm, and the castle of Kronberg, Hamlet's castle,
with its massive walls, its copper tower, and the ramparts where the ghost was said to have walked, guarded
the narrow straits through which ships sailed into the
Baltic Sea; but no beauty can compensate for deep unhappiness.

The rector spoke to Hans Christian as if he were an
idiot; when school was over, the house door was locked
and Hans Christian had to stay in the schoolroom, or
else play with the children or sit in his little room, where
he went in fear of Mrs. Meisling. Though he had been
so poor all his life, he had never lived with dirt; now
the house was filthy and untidy, the rector looked as if
he slept in his clothes, the children stank.

To Hans Christian those days in Helsingör had an
unconquerable sadness. Thoughts of his mother and himself as a child mingled in his mind. Anne Marie had had
to be put in a home. She was crippled with rheumatism
and drinking heavily; only brandy, she said piteously,
would keep out the cold; it was as if the icy water had
got into her veins. She spent every penny she was given

on the cheap raw spirits that were sold to the poor, and she had to be put under control. Everyone said she was a disgrace; Hans Christian heard them say it and had to be silent; one day he was to answer them in his story *Good-for-Nothing* and make them feel ashamed; but now he wished he could die of his loneliness and misery, and in the desolate empty schoolroom he wrote a poem.

That little poem must have taken a long time to write; its rhyme scheme was so elaborate that what Hans Christian was attempting was almost impossible, but at last it emerged whole and finished; perhaps he was slightly astounded at its simplicity—it is simple compared with the poetry of the times, especially the poetry he admired—but there was a ring in it that seemed to be true, real, as if it held a part of him.

The Dying Child has words in it that are too elaborate for the small child who speaks them—a strange fault for Andersen, but it was an unpracticed Andersen who wrote it—the talk of angels seems sentimental now, but in those days angels were a part of belief; in spite of what the critics have called "tear-stained supersensitiveness," the simplicity and pathos of the three short verses have made them famous.

> *Mother, I'm so tired, I want to sleep now;*
> *let me fall asleep and feel you near.*
> *But you mustn't cry—please, will you promise?*
> *on my face I felt your burning tear.*
> *Here's so cold, and winds outside are frightening,*

but in dreams—ah, that's what I like best:
I can see the darling angel children,
when I shut my sleepy eyes and rest.

Mother, look, the Angel's here beside me!
Can you hear how sweet the music grows?
See, his wings are both so white and lovely;
surely it was God who gave him those.
Green and red and yellow floating round me,
they are flowers the Angel came and spread.
Shall I, too, have wings while I'm alive, or—
Mother, is it only when I'm dead?

Why do you take hold of me so tightly,
put your cheek to mine the way you do?
And your cheek is wet, but yet it's burning—
Mother, I shall always be with you. . . .
Yes, but then you mustn't go on sighing;
When you cry I cry as well, you see.
I'm so tired—my eyes they won't stay open—
Mother—look—the Angel's kissing me!

"Sentimental idle rubbish," Meisling was to say when he read it, and as a punishment for having written it Hans Christian was forbidden to go out, even to church or for a walk.

After lessons the other boys could go home; he had to stay and look after the children. The squalor in the house had grown worse; he and another student boarder had to eat off the same plate. Living was dear in Helsingör, and now Meisling began complaining that the two hundred rigsdaler a year was not enough to keep an outsize lout of a boy who ate so much; Hans Christian hardly dared put a piece of meat on his plate and soon he looked as starved as in the old days in Copenhagen.

But worse than his terror of the rector, Mrs. Meisling would not leave him alone; often she brought coffee up to the two boys in the middle of the night, and once she frightened Hans Christian by coming into his bedroom in her nightgown, though she said it was only to fetch butter that she had hidden from the maids. It is fitting that this woman who cared so much what people thought should have her behavior made lastingly public.

Hans Christian was driven at last to write to Collin and beg to be taken away. His letter was hysterical but, as he could not bring himself to say a word about Mrs. Meisling, Collin, who knew the rector was bad-tempered, saw nothing more in it than usual and answered in a normal kind and sensible way that the rector really meant well and his harshness was only his manner. The letter put Hans Christian into fresh despair, but now a young teacher of Hebrew began to visit Meisling for lessons; he saw the way Hans Christian was treated, the grudged and scanty helpings of food, the five small pieces of wood allowed for his fire, the way the maids and—the young teacher could hardly believe his eyes— Mrs. Meisling embarrassed him; and in the Easter holidays this teacher made it his business to go and call on Collin. Shocked and distressed, Collin ordered Hans Christian to leave at once.

Hans Christian went to say good-by to Meisling. He

held out his hand and said, with a falseness that probably came from fright: "Thank you for all the good you have done me."

The rector was more honest. He said what he hoped. "You will never become a student," he shouted. "Your verses will rot in a bookseller's attic and you will end your days in a madhouse."

It sounded like a curse. Hans Christian had to leave with it ringing in his ears.

VIII

As there were only a few months to go before the university examination, Collin decided it was not worth
arranging for Hans Christian to go to another school;
instead he found a private tutor, a young man called
Müller, gifted but unspoiled and gentle. It was a new
experience for Hans Christian to find himself arguing
on equal and eager terms with his teacher; they argued
chiefly about religion. Müller kept rigidly to the Bible,
but Hans Christian followed his father; to Müller he
was in danger of hell fire, but Hans Christian knew he
was not; he had a child's sincere faith and he believed
with his whole heart that God was love.

It was bliss to be in Copenhagen again. He had
hired a small garret, the garret in *A Picture Book without
Pictures*; it was in one of the narrowest streets, but "light
is not wanting for me, for I live high up and I have a
fine view over the roof." So much of a writer's life is
inextricably woven with his work that it is hard to tell
what is dreamed and what is reality. Hans Christian
was then the young student poet of the story, leaning
on the sill, gazing while the moonlight shone over the
houses; he gazed until the chimney-pots seemed to
change to mountains and the gleam of the canal was a
river winding far away. The whole world came to him
there, through the moon, which said: "Paint what I tell
you, and you will have a fine picture book."

"Last evening I was gliding through the clear atmosphere of India and reflecting myself in the Ganges . . ." said the moon. "I went to a German play last night. . . ." "Yesterday I looked down upon life in Paris." "I have been in Upsala. . . ." "I have followed the polar birds and the swimming whales to Greenland." "I will give you a picture of Pompeii." And the moon brought him other, deeper thoughts of birth and death and sorrow and love. All these were waiting for him; he was nearly ready, nearly, not quite. There was still this stiff examination and Hans Christian had reluctantly to leave the moon and go back to the table where his Latin exercise lay.

To help keep expenses down he had dinner every day at one of his friends' houses; on Monday he went to the Wulffs', to the Collins' on Tuesday, the Örsteds' on Wednesday, and so on through the week.

But it was the Collin house that was his real home, and it was Edvard of whom he thought the most. Edvard was everything he, Hans Christian, was not, good-looking, controlled, modest. Hans Christian yearned to be like him. How Edvard felt it is difficult to know; he was always cool, composed, and withdrawn; in fact sometimes he behaved a little like a governess, as all the Collins did to Hans Christian; but Edvard was good-natured, he helped with the Latin compositions and the grammar that Hans Christian still found fearfully difficult. Next to Edvard it was the youngest Collin daughter, Louise, who touched him most. She had been a little girl when he first knew them; now she was fifteen and already womanly, her body full and curved, and she seemed mysterious to him. While her sister and brothers were astringent and sometimes made Hans Christian feel stupid and awkward, she was always gentle and patient.

To his friends in the capital it must have seemed that it was the same Hans Christian who came back from school each time but—was it possible?—still longer. He was nearly grown-up, over twenty-two, but he seemed to be as ebullient as ever, as brashly confident one moment, as despairing the next, as full of smiles and tears, as talkative; he still had a pocket stuffed with poems, only it was a tailcoat now, not a jacket, and he was still insistent on reading aloud.

The younger people could not bear this. "If you read, I shall go home," Edvard used to say to Hans Christian when they went out together, but sometimes Hans Christian turned the tables. Once at a party he was asked, as a joke, to read. "It's the funniest thing," the girls said, giggling together. "You will see, at the least hint, he will leap up and read." It was quite true, he did, but the poem and his way of reading it were so simple and sincere that everyone ended by clapping.

Slowly they began to see there was a change in him; in his years away Hans Christian had grown a mind filled with judgment and knowledge, and his quiet suffering under much bullying had given him dignity, a queer legacy to have come from Meisling.

People thought it was conceit that made Hans Christian read aloud; it was not, it was necessity. A poet cannot tell the effect of his poem until he has heard it,

seen its effect on an audience. It was the same later on
with the Tales; as he read them, he was listening acutely,
waiting to see where they lost pace and flagged, where
they needed more weight, and afterwards he would go
home and correct them.

Mrs. Wulff was always trying to bring him to a proper
sense of who he was. She had written to him at school,
good sensible letters: "Dear Andersen, wake up and
don't dream of becoming immortal for I'm sure you will
only be laughed at; don't dream of the poet's wreath or
of being seated among the great men. Thank God that
provision has been made so that you can learn something, that your brains can be trained . . ." and "If
I got the idea of becoming Empress of Brazil and I felt
that all my attempts went wrong, that nobody wanted
them, wouldn't I then take pains . . . to realize: 'I am
Mrs. Wulff, do your duty here and don't be a fool'?
Wouldn't the conviction prevail that it is greater to be
something less and be it well?" She talked to him here
in Copenhagen in the same way, of modesty, gratitude,
good sense, and of knowing his place; Hans Christian
tried to attend, but a moment after he would be
swept away again.

Captain Wulff often made him feel that he thought
him a waste of time, but the Wulffs' daughter, Henriette,
became his fast friend. She drew out all the tenderness
in him; she was little and hunchbacked, much more
distorted physically then he, but gay, intelligent, and
exceedingly witty, a dear companion, far closer to him
in feeling than the Collins. She shared his secrets. One

day the captain came into the drawing-room with a copy
of a newspaper, the *Flying Post*. "There is something
I want you to hear in this," he said to his wife. "Two
poems that are really good. They are signed simply 'H.'
Perhaps they are by Heiberg," and he read them aloud.
It was Henriette who said: "They are by Hans Christian."

There was a moment of surprised silence; Hans
Christian was expectantly glowing, but the captain put
down the paper and left the room as if he were vexed;
Mrs. Wulff was silent too and Hans Christian was so
hurt that presently he bowed and went home.

Mrs. Wulff had often said that if he came to Copenhagen there would be too many visits, too few lessons;
soon Hans Christian began to understand their dis-
pleasure; they thought he had been writing poetry instead of working and he had to admit it was partly
true; perhaps Meisling had been wise in forbidding it;
the examination date was close and suddenly Hans
Christian knew he would not, could not, pass. Collin
had looked grave at their last meeting and said if he
failed it was the end; they could not ask the King for
more support. Müller was looking grave too and spoke of
an extra coach for Latin. Hans Christian had never felt
his dependence more; other students, if they failed,
disappointed their parents and families, but bound up
with his results was a whole circle of benefactors; he
had the weight of that debt on him and it was dismay-
ingly public. Poems were forgotten and he worked

frantically; on the day of the examination he fainted, but he forced himself to revive, and he passed.

Although another examination, a year later, would have to be passed before a student could enter a profession, the worst was over and he, Hans Christian Andersen, had proved himself worthy of his friends, capable of difficult distasteful study, of years of toil. The sudden relief seemed to release a spring in him; to his friends it seemed that they had hardly had time to advise him what to do next when they found his thoughts had flown, "like a swarm of bees," he said, into his first book; he did not now count the efforts of William Christian Walter. It was the story of a walk. The tutor, Müller, lived in another part of the city, and in the long walks there and back Hans Christian had been at his old trick of writing in his head, as he had done long ago under his mother's apron, by the gooseberry bush; now, as if those thought-bees had been dammed up and suddenly released, they swarmed out on paper.

A *Walking Tour from Holmens Kanal to the East Point of Amager* is a jumble of all the thoughts and associations that come into the mind as the body walks along, seeing and hearing, perhaps one of the first attempts at stream-of-consciousness writing. It is a jumble of styles, too; sometimes it is in humorous verse, it has many of the stilted paragraphs that Hans Christian admired; occasionally it flows into a new style, that is quick, almost colloquial, the beginnings of the style of Hans Andersen. The whole little book was fresh and gay and unquenchably young, and everybody was charmed.

He had to publish it himself because the publishers offered such poor terms. This he did by subscription and, after extracts had appeared in the *Flying Post,* nearly the whole edition was subscribed and soon a publisher came with a good offer for a second. There was money for Collin to bank, but what made Hans Christian happier, the critics were kind.

That year everything seemed to smile on him; as if success brought success, a little vaudeville play, parody-ing those very old tragedies which he had once tried so hard to imitate, was accepted and put on for a short run at the Theater Royal. It was here he had seen *Paul and Virginia* as a penniless boy. Would his own work come to life as that had? It was on this stage that he had knelt down and prayed that New Year's Day. Now he was here again, not as an actor, but as the actor's mainspring, the playwright. Anxiety, responsibility, joy, and gratitude almost killed him.

Mrs. Collin was sitting alone that night when Hans Christian burst in on her and threw himself down into a chair, sobbing and crying. She instantly guessed what had happened. "Hush! Hush!" she soothed him. "Well-known authors, even Oehlenschläger, are often hissed."

"But they didn't hiss," cried Hans Christian. "They applauded. They cried: 'Long live Andersen!' They clapped!"

It was chiefly a student claque, but that did not cloud his joy.

That whole spring and summer were radiant. He was invited to country houses, where he joined in picnics, garden parties, singing, acting in charades. "My hardships are over," he said. It seemed that all he had to do to be happy was to write and earn a little money, and that was charming because it was writing that made him happiest of all.

Then he had a letter from Ingemann; the poet warned Hans Christian against frivolity. Ingemann knew that a social life is death to the artist, and he begged Andersen to give it up, and not to care so much for other people's opinion, but to be true to himself. Hans Christian was severely puzzled. What did Ingemann mean? Was frivolity the gay happy careless time spent in these gardens and drawing-rooms? It was true one did not talk about anything very much and the girls' laughter sounded more like bells than voices, but how could it harm him?

What is wrong with sophistication? Nothing, if it does not take one's sense of values away. Hans Andersen ended by knowing this very well. He was to write a poem, *Pjat Pjat*—"Silly Gossip"—that ruffled these very drawing-rooms, and *The Swineherd* is an ironic and delicate little indictment of society.

Growing on the grave of the Prince's father was a rose-tree—oh, such a lovely rose-tree. It only flowered every five years, and even then had but one solitary bloom. But this rose smelt so sweet that it made you forget all your cares and troubles. And the Prince also had a nightingale that could

sing just as if it had all the loveliest tunes hidden
away in its little throat. The Princess should have
both the rose and the nightingale, he said; and so
they were placed in big silver caskets and sent to
her. The Emperor had them brought before him in
the great hall . . . out came the lovely rose.

"Oh, isn't it pretty!" cried all the maids-of-
honor.

"It's more than pretty," said the Emperor, "it's
handsome."

But when the Princess touched it she nearly
burst into tears. "Oh, Papa, what a shame!" she
cried. "It's not artificial, it's real!"

"What a shame!" repeated all the court ladies.
"It's real!"

"Come, let's see what's in the other casket before we get annoyed," suggested the Emperor. And
then out came the nightingale. Its singing was so
lovely that for the moment there wasn't a thing that
could be said against it.

"*Superbe! Charmant!*" exclaimed the maids-of-
honor, for they all talked French, the one worse
than the other. "How the bird reminds me of Her
late Majesty's musical box!". . . "All the same I
can't believe that it's real," said the Princess.

"Yes, it is; it's a real live bird," said the ones
who had brought it.

"All right, then let it fly away," said the Princess
and she wouldn't hear of the Prince being allowed
to come in.

Just before Hans Christian's first university examination he had met, at dinner at the Örsteds', a young man
who was so quiet and shy that it seemed certain he must
have come from the country for the first time. "Are

you going up for the examination at the University?" Hans Christian had asked in a slightly patronizing way.

"Yes," the young man had said with a smile. Hans Christian had talked to him kindly and encouragingly and had even boasted a little, but when the day arrived and he looked among the other students, he had not been able to find the young man anywhere; he found him in the examiners' room; he was the professor who was to examine in mathematics.

More than anything else, it was the young professor's modesty and forbearance that had made Hans Christian blush most for himself; they were much the same age, one a learned professor, the other a raw boastful student, and he had vowed to try and catch up, and never to boast or idle again; Ingemann's letter made him see how badly he had broken that vow. Hans Christian tore himself away, in the middle of that summer, and went back to Copenhagen to work. He passed the examination; but, though his marks were almost brilliant, his friends were astonished to find that he said nothing about them.

IX

WITH his last examination behind him Hans Christian
Andersen felt he was no longer Hans Christian the boy,
but Andersen an avowed writer. He had a real room now,
"a heavenly blue room" he called it; the garret was gone,
there was no time for moonshine; he had dreamed away
nearly a whole year since *A Walking Trip*, his grant
from the King was finished, he had to live, and that for
an artist is always the difficulty, how to balance dreams
and living.

At Christmas he brought out the first collection of
his poems. They are of interest to us only because they
hold what is perhaps the first indication of the Tales; it
was *Dödningen—the Dead Man*—which was almost
a complete rough draft of what years later was to be
The Traveling Companion.

Mrs. Ingemann, whose big dark eyes must have seen
further than most people's, wrote to him about this poem:
"The little elves of our childhood seem to me to be,
on the whole, your good geniuses and when they live
in the fancy and heart, then, I think, there is no fear of
the stream of understanding losing itself among the glittering pebbles. I am sure the elves will show you the
right way," but Andersen had other things to think of
now. The most important critic of the day was Molbech,
sharpest and most meticulous of men; to everyone's surprise he praised the poems. "I like to listen to the sound-

ing bell of praise," said Andersen frankly, but some of the other critics seemed to find that he had lost his way among the pebbles Mrs. Ingemann wrote of, and some of them condemned the book.

It is not wise for a writer to challenge his critics, except by working steadily on, but for a very young man it is never easy to be wise, or quiet, especially anyone as thin-skinned as Andersen. He hit back violently though the Collins did their best to curb him; they said it was vanity and that he must not risk getting a name for that, but Andersen would not listen. He thought he had Molbech's approval and he had made a new friend, Mrs. Laessö, who, though she was middle-aged and had sons of her own, praised Andersen indiscriminately; after the pricks from the critics, the dry Collin remonstrances, it was soothing to be listened to as if he were Holberg himself, to have his every word treasured up and to be told he was the greatest poet of the century.

Buoyed up by Mrs. Laessö's encouragement, he decided to write a novel, such a novel that no one would be able to gainsay it; Mrs. Laessö was sure it would make a sensation. It was to be about gypsies and set in Jutland—Andersen had always wanted to see the wild heaths and marshes of Jutland—but that proved too far and expensive and he thought it had better be historical and set in the Odense he knew so well. In the early summer of 1830 he went to stay there with the widow of Iversen, the old printer, but not a word of the novel did he write.

Mrs. Iversen had her granddaughters with her, a bevy

of girls, lovely and bewitching. This was a very different femininity from Mrs. Meisling's; he was in a world of freshness, innocence, dewy beauty, curls, soft eyes, dimples, and pretty fingers. There he met Henriette Hanck, who wanted to be a writer and became his especial friend, her sister Caroline, and some pretty cousins. They played hide-and-seek in the old garden, and there seemed to be girls everywhere, peeping at him from behind bushes, girls climbing trees and showing an ankle, a petticoat, a little foot, running away from him down the old alleys, dodging behind sundials that should surely have said: "I show none but sunny hours."

The house was on the wide canal, and "near where the ships passed," he wrote in *The Story of My Life*, "was built a little battery with a wooden cannon; there was also a watch tower with a wooden soldier, all most childishly beautiful. . . ." The old garden had verses and inscriptions on its stonework that told one what to think and feel in each place, but Andersen seemed to be like the wooden soldier with no feelings at all; the beautiful girls seemed symbols, nothing else. What was the matter with him? Was he incapable of love? Then in an old castle he saw a painting of a lady and, as he gazed at it, his heart began to beat most painfully and his mouth felt dry; he could love her, if only she were alive! But she was paint and canvas. Everything seemed meaningless and silly; his heart ached unbearably, but for what? He began to think he was an imitation of a man; for him nothing was real and yet even the girls' light teasing wounded him. At last he left Mrs. Iversen and went to stay for a few days with a student friend, Christian Voigt.

The Voigts lived at Faaborg, a little town on the sea, in the beautiful south of Fyn among low hills covered with beech woods. In the bay were tiny scattered islands, the town was built with paved wharfs, streets so narrow that a cart could hardly pass along some of them, and black-beamed houses. The Voigts were rich merchants and when Andersen saw the family house he was impressed. An archway in the house itself led from the street to an immense courtyard round which warehouses were built; servants and journeymen, sailors and apprentices, buyers and sellers were going in and out; it seemed a thriving busy world with no place for a poor poet, but Christian Voigt took him in, introduced him to his eldest sister, Riborg, and at once Andersen was reassured.

It was a summer morning, the room was quiet and sunny, full of books and flowers; after the tempestuous chases at the Iversens' its quiet was balm. Riborg poured coffee and Andersen found that she could talk appreciatively of his work. He supposed she was plain; she had a wide mouth, her skin was dark, and her hair was a plain dark brown; her eyes were brown too, but he remarked how they lit up when she laughed. Looking at her portrait, at first it seems an ordinary face; but, looking deeper, it is not; it has a mature quizzical look, odd in a young girl.

She was with the two young men all day; they went

sailing and picnicked on one of the wooded islands. Andersen, of course, read aloud to them, and Riborg made a wreath of oak leaves but was too shy to offer it to him herself; she asked her brother to give it to Andersen. The next day there was another picnic and, in the evening, a dance. Andersen, who knew now he could not dance, stood like a long shadow against the wall, out of the fun until Riborg came and sat with him. They talked the evening away; it was not, he found, like other girls' talk, it was of poetry, music, philosophy, but, with the quick intelligence of a Henriette Wulff, she had the womanliness that always disturbed him and that he revered. This was no new little friend like Henriette Hanck at Odense, and he went to bed that night with his head in a tumult.

The next day Christian Voigt, beginning to guess what had happened to his friend, told him that Riborg was engaged to the son of the local apothecary; she would have been married by now but her parents did not approve. After a moment's silence, Andersen said he had better go back to Odense.

Before leaving he walked with Riborg in the garden, and told her he would call the heroine of his novel Riborg, the novel that had not been written; he picked a bunch of flowers for her and went away. When he got back to Odense he was so dreamy and abstracted that the girls laughed at him and said: "In love at last!"

"Nonsense!" he said angrily.

It had to be nonsense. What could love bring to him? What had he to offer to a Voigt? Not even as much as the apothecary's son. He saw that big rich house, the bustle of its trade, its solidity, and felt how flimsy he was. He was a poor workman's son, he had no profession, no money to study for one; there was nothing he could do but write, and what he earned from that was meager. It was not only that; Riborg was engaged to someone else.

Back in Copenhagen he tried to work. He wrote a little of the novel, then stopped and began the libretto of an opera, then collected his new poems. He wrote to Henriette Hanck in Odense: "Oh, I am sick of soul— but away with this heavy mood—it is fancy, isn't it? Now don't be angry with me because I am a bit malicious, will you? People are puzzled by my latest poems, just fancy now; they think I am in love, everyone thinks so." It was not surprising. The poems were written for Riborg; among them was *Two Brown Eyes* and such lines as:

> *You love me. I saw it in your eyes.*
> *Forget me now, it is your painful duty.*

Andersen could write to Henriette Hanck almost as easily and openly as he could talk to Henriette Wulff— he was lucky in his Henriettes—but even to her he tried to cover up his hurt; "I have already heard the names of many they are guessing at," he wrote, "some say it is Elmquist's daughter in Arhus, others that it is Countess Moltke!"—this was a joke—"others that it is Mistress Hanck in Odense! . . . and there are also some who think it is Miss Voigt. This last is really foolish as she is engaged and I could almost swear that she means no more to me than I to her. As a matter of fact we have only seen each other for a few days and she will soon be a bride. Oh, it really is a foolish world!"

Henriette, of course, saw quite easily from this that it was Miss Voigt.

On the day he heard from Christian Voigt that Riborg had come to Copenhagen, Andersen rushed to call on her; after that he went every day, always listening to every word she said and looking at her so intently that she took to blushing crimson when she saw him. Then, one evening when he left and she gave him her hand, he kissed it; for a moment he was terrified, then he saw she was not angry and he was sure she loved him. He managed to get home, though he could scarcely think for joy; now he knew that nothing mattered, not his pennilessness, nor his birth, nor his uncertain profession; all the things that had seemed such big barriers were small beside this fact of love; he was ready to give up his writing and learn a trade, or perhaps, as many poets have thought, he was sure he could do both, write and work at a trade; he did not know how things could be arranged but he knew that he must tell Riborg that he loved her.

Though she was so near he could not bring himself to go back and speak to her; instead he wrote a letter; in it he asked her, before God, to make sure she loved the other man. Her brother brought her answer. She had burst out crying, Christian said, when she read his letter. Now Andersen read hers; she wrote that she could not make the other man unhappy, they had waited and trusted so long. She must marry the apothecary's son and Andersen must try to understand.

Hans Andersen was to fall in love more than once again and each love, long afterwards, found a counter-part in one of his tales, but the one he was to write for Riborg was harsh and a little bitter. What had made her change? Was it Riborg's fault? In Faaborg the poet, the writer from Copenhagen, had seemed wonderful, but in the capital she had heard her poet laughed at, called "Lamppost," "Stork," and perhaps she had grown to be unsure. Or was it the other way round? That in spite of his protestations Andersen had secretly cooled? That in Faaborg, her own surroundings, Riborg had seemed unique, in Copenhagen she was simply provincial? *The Top and the Ball* bears out the first theory.

The ball thinks herself too good for the top. "You don't seem to realize," she says, "that my father and mother were morocco slippers and that I have cork in-side me." The ball can bounce up high, she is engaged to a swallow. . . . Long, long afterwards when the top is gilded he is accidentally thrown for a moment into a dustbin, where he finds a wrinkled old object that was once the ball. The maid comes and picks him out, the ball is left there. "The top came in for a lot of attention but nothing was said about the ball, and the top never spoke again of his old love. Love is, of course, bound to fade away when your sweetheart has spent five years in a gutter. You can't be expected to know her again if you meet her in a dustbin."

But he was not really so heartless; years afterwards, when she was happily married, he saw Riborg again. "Memories are very like amber beads," he wrote after this meeting; "if we rub them, they give back the old perfume," and when he died, a small wash-leather bag was found on his breast; in it was a letter from Riborg, perhaps the very letter in which she had refused his love; no one knows because young Jonas Collin, the grandson of old Collin, burned the letter unread. The bag is in the Odense Museum with copies of the love poems, Riborg's portrait, and a little bunch of flowers, dried now so that their colors are gone; they lie on a scrap of paper on which Riborg wrote: "from Andersen"; they are the flowers he picked for her in the garden in Faaborg.

He had only known Riborg a little while but, now he had lost her, Copenhagen felt desolate. He tried to turn to his writing but there was no comfort for him there; his second book of poems, *Fancies and Sketches*, had come out; they were sincere and perhaps deeper than anything else he had yet written, but the critics felt they had been too enthusiastic about *A Walking Trip*, not severe enough about the first book of poems, and they chose this moment to give him a general castigation. Molbech, on whom he had counted, came down and pincered him, and a clever young man only a few years older than he, Hertz, wrote scathingly of him in an article called "Letters from a Ghost," purporting to come from the dead poet Baggesen, who had talked so kindly to the small Hans Christian at that long-ago dinner at Siboni's; Hertz said Andersen had no sense of form. "Who cares about form?" Andersen growled. "It's feeling that matters," but as well as form a great many things appeared to matter.

Andersen had always been careless; old Collin, Edvard, Mrs. Wulff, even adoring Mrs. Laessö, had talked to him of trying to be more thorough, but he could not be made to see that grammar and spelling were important, he could not be bothered to look up the exact meaning of words. "If only," he said afterwards, "I had bothered to have my proofs read, paid someone to correct them; work I had not learned to do myself." Now his mistakes became public jokes.

Even amateurs thought they could teach him, but that was dangerous. One evening, in a drawing-room, a pedantic young gentleman began to pick an Andersen poem to pieces; he found flaw after flaw in line after line and, well satisfied with himself, was able to give a real lecture; when at last he put the book down, there was an impressed silence, into which the hostess's small daughter spoke. "Look," she said, pointing to the poem, "there's one little word you haven't scolded yet." The word was "and." It was almost as if Andersen were really protected by fairies.

He had other defenders; the Collins, like a real family, had been watching over him; perhaps it was Edvard who, knowing more than anyone else what was going on —after all, he had offered to correct those fatal proofs himself—now told his father that Andersen really needed help. Once more, in the familiar quiet study, the Counselor talked to Hans Christian, as he was always to be known here, and, after pondering, told him to use some of his savings and take a trip abroad.

X

JUST as the word "study" had to dawn on Hans Andersen and become a fact, a part of his life, now the word "abroad" dawned, but much faster; "abroad," "travel"; it seemed no sooner thought of than done. Among his possessions that all the world may now go to see are his traveling hat and umbrella, both well worn, and his battered valise and hatbox covered with labels.

He had always dreamed of other countries. He loved the migrant birds best of all, particularly the swallows and storks; they seemed to bring other lands close to him. Like the Viking's Wife in *The Marsh King's Daughter*, he had been awakened by the rustling of wings. "Stork on stork, sitting on the roofs and outbuildings . . . flocks of them flying round in great circles. Then all together they took off." He had never thought of going himself.

"I feel a tingling in my wings," said the Mother Stork. Andersen knew that tingling now. He would go into a new summer world where no one knew him or could bring up his past and his faults, where he could forget.

On this first trip he went no further than Germany, but he was off Danish soil and out of his little world into a big one; like the stork he could stretch his wings. He saw mountains for the first time, heard strange tongues, wandered in the great Gothic cathedrals, and saw,

for the first time too, the mystery of the Roman Cath-
olic Mass. He heard the famous choir of eunuchs in
Dresden with their exquisite treble voices.

In those days writers were not as plentiful as mush-
rooms, as they are now, and it was the custom and
courtesy, when visiting a foreign country, for an author
to call upon the authors of the land. Andersen had letters of introduction and presented himself to Tieck and
Adalbert von Chamisso. Sensitive people, artists always
responded to him. Chamisso became a real friend and
Tieck, when Andersen left, kissed him on the forehead
and wished him a poet's success. That kiss was Hans
Andersen's first acknowledgment abroad and it made him
feel at once humble and proud.

With the fervor he had brought to Shakespeare and
Walter Scott he began to read Goethe and Schiller; he
modeled poems on Heine, and he encountered some
fairy tales written by the brothers Grimm; they were not
like the usual fairy tales, and yet, he might have thought,
not quite what a fairy tale should be. If he thought at
all it was only in passing; he was too busy for fairy tales.
Soon he had returned to Copenhagen and was writing a
travel book.

"It would take an Andersen to write a travel book
after only six weeks abroad!" said the critics. They forgot
that he had once made a whole book out of a walking
trip across this very city, which most of them had lived
in all their lives and still did not see. Hans Andersen was
the perfect traveler; he had an open mind, a quick eye,
a capacity for picking up conversations and little scenes,

and a breadth of vision to wonder at great ones. The book was called *Shadow Pictures,* but there was nothing shadowy about it; he had always this uncanny power of bringing things alive, darning needles, tin soldiers, pots and pans, fir trees, but the critics refused to like it. Nothing he did pleased them and nothing was too petty for them to pounce on.

"Here is an error," said one. "Why do you write 'Dog' here with a little 'd'?" [1]

"Because I am writing of a little dog," said Andersen.

If he seemed unquenchable, it was partly unconscious; he was still very naïve; if anything was beautiful to him, he said so with enthusiasm; he thought his own works very beautiful and believed in them with his whole heart; and that heart was so big and vulnerable, it could be wounded at once; then he cried out bitterly. He knew this was not good, but he could not help it.

It was not vanity. "I wish that earlier on, when people accused me of vanity," he once told Edvard Collin, "I had had a little more self-confidence." It was because he had been made to feel inferior for so long— a poor workman's son, charity child, beggar, ignoramus —that he was so thin-skinned, thin-skinned but not really vain; really vain people like the silliest flattery; Andersen was to dislike the gushing admiration that women gave him later on, as much as he liked genuine appreciation.

Of all the critics it was Molbech who chastened him the most severely. After that one favorable review the little man changed his mind with a venom that seems

[1] In Danish, all nouns have a capital; e.g., "Dog," "Cat."

inexplicable and that recalls Meisling. Molbech was learned, pedantic, and set; he had a little vinegary spiteful face that shows his character and he vented his spite on Andersen. It was true, at that time, Andersen's writing was often bad and careless; the plays, with which he bombarded the Theater Royal, came back and a new volume of poems went unnoticed. He was writing too fast in a desperate attempt to win back his position and to keep himself, and getting further and further away from doing either.

If it is tiring to read about the continual tears, the wild happinesses, it was far more tiring to experience them; Andersen was often worn out with his own emotions, flagellated by them. A book was published in 1927 considering him as a psychiatric case, carefully considered from a doctor's point of view, but the way a poet lives is on his emotions; the soaring hopes, the deep despair are normal for a poet; for him life is very bitter or very sweet.

This was another of Andersen's bitter times. Word came from Colonel Guldberg that Anne Marie had gone quite to pieces; no one had been able to keep drink from her and now she was so violent that she had to be shut up. Andersen went to Odense but it was no use; the pitiful shambles of a woman hardly knew him. He told no one in Copenhagen about this fresh shame except Mrs. Laessö, whose uncritical kindness made him able to bare his hurts, but he starved himself to send money to his mother. Worst of all he was writing now not only against poverty but against a specter, the specter of failure. He had done nothing to show anyone that he was a genius and he had to be a genius or else he was a day-dreamer like his father, a sot like his mother, mad like his grandfather. Hour after hour he sat in his room holding his head in his hands, while the paper was blank in front of him or scribbled over with writing that was sterile, immature, mannered, still straining to be Walter Scott or Heine . . . still, still not Andersen.

XI

HANS ANDERSEN, they said, could never tell the color of a woman's eyes; "He only sees the soul in things," complained Mrs. Laessö. "If you are clever, your eyes must be brown; if you are graceful, blue!" But sometimes he could tell; in 1830 he had written a poem, *A Pair of Brown Eyes;* now, two short years later, he wrote another, *The Brown Eyes and the Blue.* The brown eyes had been Riborg's, the blue were eighteen-year-old Louise Collin's. Andersen had found he could talk to her about his unhappinesses, even about Riborg; and, as he talked, he looked at her.

All the Collins had good faces, clever foreheads, level almond-shaped blue eyes, the distinctive long straight Collin nose, and mouths that were unexpectedly sensitive and belied the severity of the rest; to Louise long silky brown hair and a very fair skin were added. "She is so white, my heart's dearest," Andersen was soon writing in another poem. It is difficult though to believe he really loved her; by her portrait in later life she looks so firmly respectable and bourgeoise, even a little ornate; but he had been hurt by Riborg, and Louise's gentleness, her nearness, her blue eyes, soon made him think he should not be talking of an old love but of a new.

Though Andersen could never have brought himself to say the word "love" to a Collin, he could pour it out in writing and he began to send Louise letters and poems that were quite unmistakable; their feeling shows in every line: "My whole life seems to me a poem and you are beginning to play quite a part in it. You are not cross about this, are you?" "Oh dear me, one need only let the heart speak to be a good poet!" He sent her *The Brown Eyes and the Blue,* and those poems that said quite plainly "heart's dearest."

Louise did not know what to do. She was a placid, solid, good girl, and she looked forward modestly to marrying, in due course, a solid average man, not a tempestuous child of a poet. She saw now where her sympathy had taken her and, with the quiet sense of old Collin, she consulted Ingeborg, who was now happily married to Adolph Drewsen. They thought of a way to curb Hans Christian without hurting his feelings and Ingeborg tactfully told him that all Louise's letters had to be shown to her married sister; this was a common practice for a young girl in 1832. That stopped the letters and poems—Andersen shrank from writing emotionally in any letter that witty, merry Ingeborg was to see—but he still haunted the house trying to catch Louise alone, only she never seemed to be alone. The blue eyes looked pityingly at him and she often seemed on the point of telling him something and drew back; then she announced her engagement to a Mr. Lind, a solicitor, solid and good like herself. No biographer seems ever to refer to him by a first name; for all time he remains "Mr. Lind."

The engagement hurt Andersen. It was not only another unsuccessful love; he had been told nothing

about it until it was public property and that made him
feel shut out; he was not after all on equal terms with
the Collins; not honored as a man and a poet.

There was reason in this feeling; the Collins were
slow temperate people; they took a long time to see
Andersen as a genius and, even when they suspected it,
they did not think it good for him to praise him. He
was someone they laughed at and scolded, as well as
protected and helped—how much they helped is to be
seen in the careful docketing and keeping of the Andersen manuscripts and letters by Edvard. They would probably have been surprised to know how much they loved
him, and so would he; even if he had known, it was not,
at twenty-eight, the sort of love he wanted from Louise,
and that she never for one moment thought of him except
as a queer adopted brother wounded him deeply. He was
not a man, he thought, but someone apart, and he was
to say of Mr. Lind: "Little Denmark has given him
more than all Europe can give this poet."

Invisible knives pressed into the Little Mermaid's
feet when she walked and no one saw them; she was
dumb and always different from the humans round her
though they loved her. "A mermaid hasn't any tears,"
wrote Hans Andersen, "and so she suffers all the more."
Today on the shores of the Langelinie her statue sits, a
small bronze figure on her rock, her face turned away
from the busy happy people on land as she gazes perpetually out to sea. She looks ineffably lonely and she
might be called the statue of Andersen's heart.

He knew he must hide his grief and he could think

of only one way to do it; when he had been unhappy before, old Collin had advised him to go away; he wanted now to get away to the ends of the earth. He was advised to present one of his books to King Frederik and, if it were accepted, to ask the favor of a stipend for traveling. Andersen thought that monstrous. "What, give a book and at once ask a favor!"

It was Collin who put things more sensibly. "The King is a very busy man," he said. He would rather you showed that indelicacy than bother him with a second interview."

All the same Andersen could hardly do it. "Well, where is your petition?" the old King asked bluntly when he had accepted the book.

"I have it here," said Andersen, but he was so ashamed that out gushed his tears. "It seems to me so dreadful that I should bring it with the book," he said. "They told me it was the only way, but it is not like me."

The King's gruffness disappeared; he laughed and took the petition and Andersen was granted a stipend for two years instead of the customary one.

There were not many countries in 1832 that gave their artists and writers grants for travel without asking for any specific return. Andersen had no clear idea of what he wished to do. His heart was unbearably sore but he began to find renewed proof of the friendship the Collins felt for him. They felt Andersen had come to a point of culmination from which he must begin again. He was only twenty-eight but he had had two bitter love affairs and he had come full tilt against the critics. It was better, they told him, that he should be forgotten for a little while and come back fresh. He himself felt he could hardly go on living. "I prayed . . . I might die away from Denmark," he wrote, and then, with a flicker of his real self, "or else return strengthened in activity to win for me and my beloved ones joy and honor."

All the Collins came to see him off and, on the ship, as Copenhagen fell away, the captain brought him a letter and said, laughing: "It came just now through the air." It was a letter Edvard had given him for Andersen and it said more than the distant contained Edvard had ever said:

Monday noon, April 22, 1833

Dear Friend! Suddenly the idea struck me that it might please you to receive a letter from me before you reached Hamburg and before you could expect a letter. Believe me, I'm intensely sorry at your departure, I shall miss you dreadfully; I shall miss you coming up to my room to talk to me; on Tuesdays I'll miss you on your seat at the table; still, I know, you will miss more, for you are alone; but, true, it is a consolation to know that one has friends back home who think of one, so you have this consolation, for we shall constantly remember you with love. Good-by, my dear, dear friend! God let us meet again glad and happy in two years.

XII

ANDERSEN, in Paris, had never really left Denmark; every day he waited at the post office for letters from home and, like most people abroad, he had found out his own countrymen; with other Danes he made a company so close that they all lived in the same hotel, went together to cafés, restaurants, and theaters, and always spoke their own language.

He longed for letters and none came. "Just fancy," he wrote to Christian Voigt, "I have written twenty-one letters to people in Copenhagen and no reply at all!" Not a line from Edvard, or Henriette Hanck or Henriette Wulff or Mrs. Laessö. Then one morning there was a fat letter for him; the postage was unpaid but he paid it eagerly and found that the envelope held nothing but a newspaper in which there was a hideous lampoon of himself; it seemed a token of what Denmark felt for him and he began to eschew his Danish friends and go about more, and alone, in Paris.

He went to see Cherubini, to whom he had brought some music from his old patron, the composer Weyse. Cherubini "looked like the pictures I have seen of him," he wrote; "he sat before the piano with a cat on each shoulder." Andersen met Victor Hugo and recorded that the great man was dressed in a bedgown, drawers, and a pair of elegant boots.

The Royal Library in Copenhagen has a book it particularly prizes, Hans Andersen's Album, about which he wrote: "It accompanied me on all my travels and has since increased and become of great value to me." Andersen asked Victor Hugo for his signature, but Hugo was suspicious of this young foreigner. Thinking a bill or an assignment might be written over his name, he wrote "Victor Hugo" at the extreme top of a sheet of paper, right in the corner; Andersen understood and it stung, but he pasted the sheet in his Album; it can be seen there today.

As well as keeping the Album, he made small pen and ink sketches of the places he visited, each little drawing as vivid and alive as everything he touched; they make one wonder why he did not illustrate his travel books.

It was on this first visit to Paris that he visited Versailles and saw Napoleon's bedroom. He went to the Opéra and the theater; he was at the unveiling of the Napoleon column and saw the King, Louis Philippe, and his pale Queen Amélie, who appeared to be terrified of the Parisian crowd, as she might well be.

This was the quick fiery Paris of the restoration. The prosaicness of Napoleon's military rule was over; the gilt eagles, the heavy furnishings had disappeared; the nobles with all their taste and elegance had come into power again, the arts flourished. Life in Paris was stimulating, impromptu, extravagant, loose, and gay; it must have been heady for Andersen, coming from the restraint and simplicity of Denmark, but soon not all its great men, its gaiety and good company, fireworks and theaters could hold him. He was a writer and there was something he wanted to write, something he had to write, and he needed quiet. "If you would condescend to visit a little town high up in Switzerland, where it snows even in August, you would find a cheap place," a Swiss friend told him, and Andersen went to Le Locle in the mountains.

Switzerland was more wonderful to him than Paris. There are no mountains in Denmark, and when the first views of the Alps opened in the mists, they seemed to Andersen like forms swimming high up in the air. What he had thought was a thick smoke came curling upwards to the coach, it was a cloud; they were traveling above the clouds and then: "through an opening in the mountains we saw far below a deep lovely green, a land such as you see in your dreams; it was Geneva, its lake as clear as the azure sky. There runs the Rhone, so blue that the water itself seems colored. The mountains stood high over the horizon like waves of violet glass tipped with creamy foam." It might have been the country of the Ice Maiden.

He found the Swiss friendly and hospitable; when he arranged to live with a French family in the little watch-making town, they would not hear a word about payment. "It is an invitation," they said. There were two old aunts, Rosalie and Lydia, who mended and knitted for him, and the children grew so fond of him that they used to shout their dialect in his ears; they could not believe that such a sympathetic man could not understand them.

The clouds often floated below the house; there was stillness and rest in the dark pine trees standing round it, in the big forests that led away; there was beauty in the bright green grass and the juicy violet-colored crocus; there was peace in which to write his poem, the poem that haunted him and that he had begun in Paris.

It was the story of an old Danish folk song, *Agnete and the Merman*. Even as a child the old story of the double world of earth and sea had taken hold of him; it was, of course, the first seed of *The Little Mermaid*, but the fairy tale was still a long way off and Andersen was trying the theme now as a long elaborate poem; he sent it home before leaving Le Locle for Italy. "*Agnete* is Danish in soul and mind," he wrote in the preface. "I send my dear child to my motherland, where she belongs. My friends, receive her kindly."

Agnete might be said to be Andersen's best dramatic work; the dialogue is poor, but the whole is strong and tragic; not an unworthy sister of *The Little Mermaid*, but no one received her kindly. "My ugly child," he called her afterwards. When he reached Milan he was surprised to get a cross letter from Edvard, and one even more severe at Rome. No one liked the poem, no publisher would take it; Edvard was trying to get it printed by private subscription but no one would subscribe. "Is *he* writing again?" they said. "We were tired of him long ago." Edvard managed to get it printed in the end, but he suggested with asperity that this really should be the end and Andersen's silly writing be given up.

Andersen felt he could almost throw his pen into the

Tiber and himself after it, almost but not quite; to a writer it is the book or the poem he is writing, that is coming to him now, in which he is interested; the one that is gone is dead. Of course no one likes to have disrespect shown to the dead, and any writer resents unkind criticism, but it is the living book to which he is bound; Andersen survived the attacks that were to be made on *Agnete* because he was writing something else. "*Agnete* and Le Locle," he said afterwards, "closed one part of my life."

If Germany is the country of the heart, France of common sense, Italy is the land of imagination, and in it Andersen breathed with an ease and happiness he had never known before. There was a quality in him that the North had chilled and stilled; now it was released and everything seemed larger, warmer, more free. "Come with me," says the swallow in *Thumbelina*, "come across the mountains to the warm countries," and when at last they were reached,

> . . . the sun was shining there far more brightly than with us and the sky looked twice as far. On walls and slopes grew the finest black and white grapes, in the woods hung lemons and oranges; the air smelt sweetly of myrtle and curled mint, and the most delightful children darted about the roads playing with large gay-colored butterflies. But the swallow kept flying on and on and the country became more and more beautiful. . . .

Andersen went to Milan and Genoa, but it was in Florence that he seemed to get new eyes. Not since he

had dreamed about that little landscape on the door panel at home in Odense had he looked, really looked, at paintings and sculpture; now as he looked at these Michelangelos and Botticellis, at David and Perseus and the Medici Venus, of which he wrote: "The marble has looked into my soul," it seemed, not as if he went into them, as he used to go into the panel, but they into him. Now he understood what he had refused to understand before, the necessity of form, and he saw how blind he had been. He said of that time: "The snow melted away before my eyes and a new world of art opened," and he wrote home: "I wish I were just seventeen years old and had the same sentiments and ideas as now; I would surely become something; now I only see that I don't know anything, and life is so short; how can I possibly learn so enormously much? That is a sensation I have never known; it makes me intensely sad!"

But he was catching up, growing more than he knew, and what Florence had begun, Rome completed.

No one who has seen the vastness of Rome can be small again, and Andersen lived there for four months. Even the first sad news of *Agnete*, and the worse that followed of its printing and reception, which was as bad as even Edvard had feared, could not stop his growth; he was learning to take those criticisms better though his susceptibility could still be keenly wounded, and he had a friend, an artist, met here in Rome, who could calm him as Ingemann used to do at Sorö; it was the Danish sculptor Thorvaldsen, with his wide attractive face like a dreaming lion's, and his passion for his work. "Tie my

hands behind my back and I shall bite the marble better than you can chisel it," he said once to a rival.

Thorvaldsen's works are among the treasures of Denmark; they are to be seen chiefly in the Thorvaldsen Museum at Copenhagen and in the cathedral that has the well-known statue of Christ above the altar, the huge figures of the twelve apostles down the aisles, and a font of a kneeling angel holding a mussel shell, in which most of the city's babies are baptized. Thorvaldsen's work may now look massive, too plain and lifelike to be interesting to those who are used to modern angles; there is nothing unexpected in it but, as one looks at it, the feeling of restfulness and dignity grows.

The man was like his work; when Edvard sent Andersen the first bad reviews of *Agnete*, Andersen rushed with them to Thorvaldsen, who, when he had read them, spoke seriously to the younger man. "Never let this sort of thing touch you," he said. "Feel your own strength. Don't be led by popular opinion. Go quietly ahead. Peace of mind is essential to creative work. You are unfortunate in needing a public, but this is something one must never be aware of or one becomes the prey of its whims."

He made Andersen feel strong enough to match that advice; and when Andersen left Rome for Naples, it was with one of the most severe of his former critics, someone from whom, not long before, he would have run away, the very Hertz who, in "Letters from a Ghost," had castigated him for lack of form. Old Collin had written and told Andersen that Hertz was com-

ing to Italy and had suggested they make friends; old
Collin was always wise and in this new, propitious atmosphere Andersen began to write his first novel.

He felt fresh and full of life, almost too full of life.
Everywhere was this languorous, careless, tempting
beauty. "From Cicero's villa," he wrote in his diary,
"we saw the Garden of the Hesperides. I strolled in the
warm air under the lemon and orange trees and threw
the shining yellow fruit into the blue sea." At night they
saw Vesuvius against the moonlit sky and came down
to Portici talking of poetry and of eating—they were
very hungry and every *osteria* was shut—while the
houses shone in the moonlight and scents from unknown
gardens filled the night.

It was not only the beauty. In his years of study, of
writing and poetizing, Andersen had lost touch with
people, the ordinary people he had known as a child in
Odense, as a boy in Copenhagen; now, as he traveled,
he began to find them again; the people he met did not
know he was a writer, they discovered themselves to him
unconsciously; he seemed to see into the lives of hus-
bands and wives, old maids, seamen, inn servants, beg-
gars; they seemed to be asking for his attention and he
thought often of his old home; then he had a letter from
Collin telling him that Anne Marie had died.

Andersen's first thought was: "God I thank Thee.
Now her poverty is at an end," but soon he began to
feel utterly alone; there was no one now whom he could
call his own. Everybody round him had someone, a
mother, father, children, a wife; it was the wives he

watched most of all and these lively black-eyed Italian women were attractive. In Rome he had seen a model with her breasts naked; he was haunted by the thought of her and here in Naples he saw a girl, almost a child, in rags but with violets in her black hair, beautiful as a statue; she came up to him and gave him flowers.

"My blood is in a strong commotion," he wrote in his diary. "I feel a tremendous sensuality, and I fight with myself. Is it really a sin to satisfy this powerful lust? Then may I fight it. So far I'm innocent but my blood burns, when dreaming my whole being boils. The South claims its rights. I'm half sick. Lucky is he who is married, is engaged! Oh, were these strong ties on me! But I shall fight this weakness. . . ."

With all his dreams, his romance, that is what Andersen wanted, a wife. His body was awkward but it was passionate and strong. It ached for fulfillment but it was fastidious. As many ugly men do, he could have found women over and over again, but not the delicacy and beauty that drew him; if he could not have that, he wanted nothing else and he tried to bear the torment of longing: "Thought of Louise and the others at home; if they had seen me last night, they would surely have been afraid of me. Naples is more dangerous than Paris, for there one is cold, but here the blood burns."

The kind of women he wanted, the Louise Collins, hardly thought of him as a man, they were fond of the child in him. It was the price he paid for his gift; one of the qualities of Andersen's writing, the one that makes it impossible for anyone to imitate him, is its purity of feeling, its innocence; it is like the pure clear voice of the choristers he had heard in Dresden, who had given up their manhood to sing. "All for that?" he had asked after listening to the eunuch choir, but without surprise. The singing was worth it. Yes, all for that! and the last entry in the diary of this time is on March 20: "Innocent I left Naples after all."

He came home through Italy, by Vienna and Munich, traveling slowly to his familiar place. He did not want to come home; he thought he knew what was waiting for him there, criticism, antagonism, that perpetual good advice, but it had to be faced, his stipend had run out; not quite three hundred dollars had lasted him for sixteen months. "His economy," said Collin, "was one of his greatest talents," but the last penny had now been spent. "So tomorrow I travel towards the north. A strange sorrowful feeling possesses me. Northward, there where my dear ones live in snow and fog, lies the iron ring to be fastened to my foot."

There was one thing that brought him a feeling of hope—his novel. He finished the first part in Ingemann's house at Sorö, where he was given a little room high up in the roof on a level with the fragant lime trees. Ingemann was always a good influence and the work went well. The second part was finished in Copenhagen, where he had taken rooms in the Nyhaven, on the sunless side because it was cheaper. "A cold shadow lies over my study," he wrote in a letter to Henriette Wulff, who was away in the Italy he mourned, "but outside I see pennants and sails. The ships come and go in the green waters of the canal, once in a while the waves nod their heads; when the moon shines on them, they have something wistful to tell from when they shone on sulphurous fire in the Blue Grotto, had pink cheeks in the glare of Vesuvius. In the garden stands a tall, leafy poplar; by moonshine it looks quite black; then I recall the dark cypresses and all the beautiful things I dreamt of the other day. Yes, I have dreamt so clearly that I was in Italy last year, so I must write my Italian story, exhale all that I dreamt and saw."

Soon he was able to put the two parts together and inscribe them "To the Conference Counselor Collin and his noble wife, in whom I found parents, whose children were my brothers and sisters, whose house was my home, I present the best that I possess." It was not only the best; at that moment it was all he possessed in the world, his only asset.

Edvard took the novel to a publisher and bargained for his friend. Twenty pounds was all the publisher would give, and in installments only, but Andersen accepted. He had to accept; he had not paid his rent for a month, and though his daily dinner was still given him by his friends, he had no decent clothes or shoes.

Because he was so poor, so short of money, while he was waiting for *The Improvisatore*, as he had called the novel, to go through the press, he wrote a little pamphlet, four fairy tales for children.

XIII

THOSE first fairy tales were *The Tinder-Box*, *Little Claus and Big Claus*, *Little Ida's Flowers*, and *The Princess and the Pea*, three adapted from folk tales, but all of them were told in Andersen's own way. He sent them to Henriette Wulff to read—*The Princess and the Pea* was really a dig at her, who was so fussy over small things. "Ōrsted says that if *The Improvisatore* will make me famous, these will make me immortal, but that of course I don't believe," he said.

All his hopes were on the novel. *The Improvisatore* is the story of a poor boy, an improviser of poems and tales, in fact Andersen himself, but called Antonio and living not in Denmark but in Italy. The transition into that warm sunny land seemed to have released a spring in him and he wrote this, his real autobiography, far more truthfully and deeply than he wrote the straight-forward *Story of My Life*; the characters are all people who were part of him—his mother, his mad grand-father, Meisling, Mrs. Meisling, his teachers in Copen-hagen. It was vitally important to him; without it he would never have sloughed off the last of that poor fum-bling ignorant boy, that perpetual student, and emerged, free, as Hans Andersen. The descriptions of Italy were beautiful; they hold their beauty even now when Vic-torian descriptions seem tedious reading, and the book, while it kept the freshness of *A Walking Trip*, had a form and pace which were new. It was in its way a momentous book; it made a revolution in the history of the Danish novel, and it was the turning-point of his life.

He waited with sickening anxiety for it to come out, but there was nothing that need have made him afraid; indeed, for a while "nothing" seemed the right word. There were few reviews, but he had not expected many and, while the critics who did review it still moralized, they could not help being favorable. There was a new feeling in the air; it was approval, something Andersen had not felt for a long time. His most candid friends were pleased, the Collins, Henriette Wulff; and some of the approval was from men whose opinion he prized most, Hertz, Ingemann, and even Hauch, a critic who had despised him openly before; Captain Wulff, who had been so ungraciously silent long ago about the poems in the *Flying Post*, told everyone: "I couldn't put the book down!"

It ran into several editions, it was translated into Swedish and German, and into English by Mary Howitt, who became an Andersen enthusiast. No wonder he was pleased, and, being Andersen, "pleased" meant "cockahoop." Before the year was out he had finished another novel, *O.T.*, and begun yet another. "I want to be the first novelist of Denmark," he said. "Modest as ever!" groaned the Collins.

But even Andersen knew that such things will not come of one's own volition. Among his last tales is a little one called *The Pen and the Inkpot*. ". . . It is wonderful what a number of things can come out of me

. . . [said the inkpot]. It's quite incredible. And I really don't know myself what will be the next thing, when that man begins to dip into me. . . . From me all the works of the poet go forth."

"You only furnish the fluid," said the pen. ". . . It is the pen that writes. No man doubts that; and, indeed, most people have almost as much insight into poetry as an old inkstand."

"You've but little experience," replied the inkpot. "You've hardly been in service a week, and are already half worn out. Do you fancy you are a poet? You are only a servant; and before you came I knew many of your sort, some of the goose family and some of English manufacture. . . . I know the quill, as well as the steel pen. Many have been in my service . . . and I shall have many more when he comes—the man who goes through the movements for me, and writes down what he draws from me. . . ."

The pen and the inkpot got so angry with each other in their claims as to who really made the poet's work that they were obliged to call each other names.

"Ink-pipkin!" cried the pen.

"Writing-stick!" cried the inkpot.

"But the poet knew it was only God who made the poem. . . ." And God, in life, has a way of giving you what you want in such a curious fashion that you do not recognize it. "I shall be famous," Hans Andersen had said all his life, and when the fame began to come he hardly saw it.

He was busy with his novels. *O.T.* was a poor dashed-off thing but he had made a name with *The Improvisa-tore* and the new book was not badly received. It did not sell well though, and as all the children he met seemed to know his first book of tales, and it at any rate was selling, he wrote a second. Among the new stories was *Thumbelina*. Like *The Princess and the Pea*, it was written for tiny, witty Henriette Wulff. How many little girls, some of them great-grandmothers now, have read that story and floated miniature dolls on water-lily or nasturtium leaves, or made walnut-shell cradles with vio-let pillows and flower-petal counterpanes? Countless thousands, but "Really I should drop these trifles," said Andersen, "and concentrate on my real work."

He still did not dream what that was, but slowly he began to be aware of something that was slightly dis-concerting; people had begun to point him out in the street, which pleased him very much, to talk to him; but though it was often as the author of that charming Italian novel, it was far more often as the man who wrote the Tales; shop people recognized him and children were stopped by their mothers and nurses and told: "Look, there is your Hans Andersen."

He was easy to recognize. As soon as he made a lit-tle money he took great care of his appearance. He had always loved clothes from the day when his friends filled him with joy by giving him their secondhand ones; now he had a coat lined with velvet and a tall hat, and his hair was curled by a hairdresser. It was part of his naïveté, his friends smiled at it, but it was also an attempt to get away as far as possible from the wooden shoes, the rags and patches and the shame of desperate makeshifts, such as padding out that coat front with programs.

Elith Reumert, who wrote a loving study of Andersen in *Andersen, the Man*, gives a description of how, as a boy, he once saw Andersen in Copenhagen:

> I was a lad of fourteen when, one day, on my way to school, I saw a tall and peculiar figure turning the corner . . . whom I, at once, from the many pictures I had seen, recognized as Hans Christian Andersen . . . the poet. When he passed me I stood at attention and instinctively took off my cap most respectfully. To my surprise he returned my salute with such excessive politeness that I felt quite shy. He gave me a pleased and kindly smile and when he slowly passed on, backwards, I was afraid he would stumble over his own legs. He kept swinging his hat towards me, nodding and smiling, until he disappeared.
>
> As I stood there I felt as if I was in a dream . . . to tell the truth I was not quite sure he had not been making fun of me.
>
> Now I know better. He, who could be made happy by a friendly word or depressed by a hard one; he who with astonishing honesty had confessed to the world that his soul only felt happy when admired by everyone . . . he had, in the street, met with one of those youngsters who in deep veneration and gratitude had paid him a child's homage, and in his childlike heart he felt, at the moment, this homage as a great joy.
>
> . . . What I most distinctly remember was his loving smile, which lighted up his whole face and beautified his plain coarse features . . . he was

not like anyone I had ever seen and I felt that this was as it should be. . . . The extraordinary proportions of his body made his movements awkward, but in all their awkwardness they were as pleasing to me as a young foal. The helplessness of a child and the huge form of a man . . . were indeed a quaint contrast. And I noticed one thing besides . . . the simply fantastic width of his trousers.

XIV

IT often seems that children have a telegraphic system of their own, without any wires or delivery forms; a fashion spreads among them—in Andersen's day it would have been conkers or hoops or marbles, today a space helmet, a Nancy-Anne doll or frog swimming feet—one day none of the children seems to have a certain thing, the next it is everywhere and every boy or girl has adopted it. The Andersen Tales spread quickly, first over Denmark, then into Germany, on to Sweden, England, and over the world.

But they were to be more than a fashion and soon they were found on the grownups' tables as well as in the nursery. That is what Andersen had meant: "I get hold of an idea and tell a story for the young ones," he said, "remembering all the time that father and mother are listening and we must give them something to think about too." The result was beyond anything he had expected but, when he brought out the third collection of Tales and Heiberg, an author himself and the most sophisticated of critics, declared *The Little Mermaid* and *The Emperor's New Clothes* to be the best things H. C. Andersen had ever written, Andersen was completely bewildered.

The Little Mermaid better than *Agnete*? Though it was true that nothing he ever wrote moved him as much while writing as the fairy tale, it was written in a few days, while the poem took months of work. He was not only mystified, he was a little annoyed.

People who have not read Andersen may ask, with him, what there was in these little tales that has placed them where they are. Why these? What is it that makes them so different from Perrault or Grimm? The answer is "everything."

To begin with, they have a perfection of form that none of the others achieved; it astonished even Hertz. Each story has the essence of a poem, and a poem is not prose broken into short lines, but a distilling of thought and meaning into a distinct form, so disciplined and finely made, so knit in rhythm, that one word out of place, one word too much, jars the whole. In Andersen we are never jarred and it is this that gives the Tales their extraordinary swiftness—too often lost in translation—so that they are over almost before we have had time to take them in, and we have had the magical feeling of flying. The children, he remarked, always had their mouths a little open when he had finished; that is the feeling we have too.

But they were not written swiftly, were not the happy accidents that some people think them; anyone who has studied the original manuscripts from the first short draft of a story, through all its stages of crossings out, rewritings and alterations in Andersen's small spiky handwriting, the cuttings and pastings together, until the last draft was ready for the printer, can see how each word was weighed, and what careful pruning was done, what discipline was there. Even the discipline was skillful; Andersen never let it kill the life in his style.

That life is his hallmark. A sentence from one of Hans Andersen's Tales is utterly different from a sentence by anyone else. "The children got in the coach and drove off," Perrault or Grimm would have written, but Hans Andersen wrote: "Up they got on the coach. Good-by, Mum. Good-by, Dad. Crack went the whip, whick whack and away they dashed. Gee up! Gee up!"

"It's not writing, it's talking," the irritated Molbech had said, but, one after another, serious literary critics have found in it a source of inspiration: "From that moment," said Jacobsen, "a new prose was born in Danish literature; the language acquired grace and color, the freshness of simplicity."

That is what is lost, most of all, in English translations. The newest, by R. P. Keigwin, catch it, the Danish scholars say, as never before, but to American and English people, brought up on the sentimental verbose Andersens we have all known, these may come as a surprise. "But he makes the kitchen-maid in *The Nightingale* say 'Gosh!' " said one American critic. Precisely, because "Gosh" is nearest to the Danish of what she did say. "Where is your spunk?" the witch asks the Little Mermaid. That critic would no doubt have preferred: "Where is your courage?" but "spunk," its one syllable snapped out so quickly, is nearer to Andersen. The difference in translations can be shown by studying the story of *The Tin Soldier*. He has been called "The Dauntless Tin Soldier," "The Constant," "The Steadfast"; Mr. Keigwin uses "The Staunch." That small taut firm word "staunch" is exactly right for a little tin soldier and it has the quickness and economy of the Danish. With all their slang, the stories keep their beauty; Andersen is one of the few writers who use slang beautifully.

In the Bible we are told that God formed Man out of the dust of earth and breathed into his nostrils . . . and Man became a living soul. Without irreverence it might be said that Hans Andersen did something like that too; he formed his stories of the dust of earth: a daisy, an old street lamp, a darning needle, a beetle, and made them live. His breath was unique; it was an alchemy of wisdom, poetry, humor, and innocence.

He was adult, a philosopher, and a lovable man; his stories are parables and have meanings that sound on and on—sometimes over our heads—after their last word is read. He was a poet and knew the whole gamut of feeling from ecstasy to black melancholy and horror. People call him sentimental; in a way he was, but in the first meaning of the word, which is not "excess of feeling" but an abounding in feeling and reflection. He was a child; children have this godlike power of giving personality to things that have none, not only toys, but sticks and stones, banister knobs and footstools, cabbages; it dies in them as they grow up, but Andersen never lost this power. "It often seems to me," he wrote, "as if every hoarding, every little flower is saying to me: 'Look at me, just for a moment, and then my story will go right into you.' " "Right into you," that is the clue. The daisy, the street lamp, the beetle—they are suddenly breathing and alive.

Once upon a time there was a bundle of matches; they were tremendously proud of their high birth. Their family tree—that's to say, the tall fir tree that each little match-stick came from—had been a huge old tree in the wood. And now the matches lay on the shelf between a tinder-box and an old iron cook-pot, and they told the other two about the time they were young. "Ah, yes," they said, "in those days, with the velvet moss at our feet, we really were on velvet. Every morning and evening we had diamond tea; that was the dew. And all day we had sunshine. . . . But then the woodcutters arrived; that was the great upheaval, and our family was all split up. Our founder and head was given a place as mainmast on board a splendid ship that could sail round the world if she liked; the other branches went to other places and, as for us, we've got the task of lighting up for the common herd; that's how we gentlefolk come to be in the kitchen."

"Well, things have gone differently with me," said the cook-pot which stood alongside the matches. "Right from the time I first came into the world, I've been scrubbed and boiled again and again. I've got an eye for the practical and, strictly speaking, I'm No. 1 in this house. My great delight, at a time like after dinner, is to sit clean and tidy on the shelf and have a nice little chat with my friends. But except for the water-bucket, who now and then goes down into the yard, we spend all our time indoors. Our one news-bringer is the market basket, but that goes in for a lot of wild

talk about the government and the people. Why,
the other day there was an elderly jug so flabber-
gasted by what the basket said that it fell down and
broke in pieces. It's a real radical, that basket,
mark my words!"

"How you do chatter!" said the tinder-box; and
the steel let fly at the flint, so that it gave out sparks.
"Come on, let's have a cheerful evening!"

"Yes, let's discuss who belongs to the best family," said the matches.

"No, I don't like talking about myself," said the
earthenware jar. "Let's have a social evening. I'll
begin. . . . On the shores of the Baltic, where
the Danish beech trees . . ."

"It does sound interesting the way you tell it,"
said the broom. "One can hear at once that it's a
lady telling the story; there's such a refined note
running through it all."

"That's just how I feel," said the bucket, and it
gave a little hop of sheer delight, and that meant
"splash!" on the floor. Then the cook-pot went on
with its story, and the end was every bit as good as
the beginning.

The plates all rattled with joy, and the broom
took some green parsley out of the bin and crowned
the cook-pot with it, knowing this would annoy the
others and "if I crown her today," she thought,
"then she'll crown me tomorrow."

"Now I'm going to dance," said the tongs, and
dance she did—my word, what a high kick! The
old chintz on the chair in the corner fairly split himself looking at it. "Now may I be crowned?" asked
the tongs, and crowned she was.

"After all, they're the merest riffraff," thought
the matches.

It is a whole live kitchen world. After reading it a kitchen never seems the same place again; one is almost afraid to take a shopping basket out for fear of what it might think; it is almost as if the dustpan might speak; and notice in how few words it is told. All the stories have this economy, this startlingly quick effect. None of them, except *The Snow Queen*, which is almost a novel, is long; Andersen is verbose and boring in his novels and autobiography, but these are his poems—for that is what he always was, a poet.

Not everyone approved. There were some bad reviews. "Although the reviewer has nothing against good fairy tales for grownups," said one, "he can only find this form of literature entirely unsuitable for children . . . ought their reading, even out of school, to be merely for amusement? . . . Far from improving their minds," he said severely, "Andersen's Tales might be positively harmful. Would anyone claim that a child's sense of what is proper would be improved when it reads about a sleeping Princess riding on the back of a dog to a soldier who kisses her? . . . or that its sense of modesty be improved by reading about a woman who dined alone with a sexton in her husband's absence? Or its sense of value of human life after reading *Little and Big Claus*? As for *The Princess and the Pea* it is not only indelicate but indefensible, as the child might get the false idea that great ladies must be terribly thin-skinned. . . ." The critic ended by saying: "*Little Ida's Flowers* is innocent, but it has no moral either."

We smile at such criticism, but there are others that

threaten Andersen just as seriously; for instance, there is an idea now that children should be given books without shadows, books of brightness and lightness, and laughter, nothing else; perhaps the reason why these books are so lifeless is that living things have shadows.

Andersen had his dark side, a legacy from his horror of his grandfather, from the woman who tried to pin him in the lunatic cell, from the prison, and the tales with which Anne Marie and the spinning women had frightened him as a little boy and, more especially, from the customs of his time. One must remember he was writing in the first half of the nineteenth century and had spent his own childhood among ignorant, crude, and superstitious people; once he had dipped his pen in ink, both of which after *The Pen and the Inkpot* seemed despotically alive, he was carried on to the end.

Stories as vividly horrid as *The Girl Who Trod on a Loaf*, as sad as *The Shadow*, should perhaps be kept away from children altogether, but to expunge parts of them, to tell them in another way, is to destroy them, and that is desecration, not too strong a word; and almost always it is safe to trust to the children. Andersen's *The Little Mermaid* has terrible parts, the story is one of the saddest on earth, but it is also one of the very best loved.

In pictures and statues of Andersen, tiny children are shown listening to the stories. This is sentimentally false; the stories were not meant for tiny children. In Andersen's time, very little children were kept in the nursery when visitors came to the house; it was not until they were eight or nine years old that they were allowed to go down to the drawing-room or in to dessert to meet Mr. Hans Andersen and perhaps hear his Tales. Even then they did not understand the whole; they were not meant to; all Andersen wanted was that they should love them; presently, as they grew up, they would understand; to stop and explain—as conscientious mothers do —is to spoil the rhythm, the whole feeling. Let the children wonder; these are wonder tales.

How completely Andersen understood children can be seen by his letters to his child friends; he knew, to a nicety, what would please them at all ages.

When little Maria Henriques was four years old he wrote to her from the seaside:

June 7, 1870

My sweet little Marie!

I am—as you are—staying in the country. You are at Petershoi, but I am far on the other side of Copenhagen, at the forest and the sea, like you. Here it is so lovely. And I have got strawberries, big red strawberries with cream. Have you got that? They are tasting right down in the stomach.

Then I sit down on a stone down by the sea, then suddenly a big white bird comes flying, a gull; it flies right down against me so that I believe it will beat me with its wings, no, good gracious, it said: "Ma! Ma! —ri!"

"I beg your pardon?" I asked; "Ma! Ma!—ri!" it said again.

And then I understood that Ma! Ma!—ri! means "Marie!"

"*Well!*" I said, "*is it Marie from whom you are greeting me?*"

"*Ja! Ja!*" [*in Danish, "Yes! Yes!*"] "*Ma, ma, ri,*" it said.

It couldn't say it any better. It only understood gull language, and this is not much like our manner of speaking.

"*Thanks for the greetings!*" I said and then the gull flew away.

Then, as I was walking up in the garden came a little sparrow. "*You've been flying about so far, so far, I imagine,*" I said.

"*Vidt, vidt*" [*in Danish, "Far, far*"], it said.

"*Have you been at Petershoi?*" I asked.

"*Lidt, lidt, lidt*" ["*A little, a little, a little*"], it said.

"*Did you see Marie?*" I asked.

"*Tidt, tidt, tidt*" ["*Often, often, often*"], it said.

"*Then you are going there again, I suppose?*" I said. "*Then give my greetings to Marie.*"

"*Lidt, lidt*" ["*A bit, a bit*"], it said.

Hasn't it been with you yet? Then it will come later, but first I will send you a letter.

It's nice to be in the country, to go bathing, to eat something or other [*note: in Danish these make three rhymes*], *and to have a letter from your sweetheart.*

H. C. Andersen

Little Marie treasured that letter and kept it all her life. Children are the quickest judges and the clamor for stories, more stories, that rose from them is the answer to all criticism.

"It is easy," Andersen was to say of the Tales. "It is just as you would talk to a child. Anyone can tell them." Time has made it very plain that no one can tell them but Hans Andersen.

XV

IT is not a happy thing to be a writer; it may sound an easy life but it is not; imagination is the writer's greatest gift but it can be torture in everyday life. A poet for instance is unpredictable even to himself; he never knows when or how his ecstasy or melancholy will seize him; it has nothing or little to do with outside circumstances; the same people, the same place, the same things can fill him with joy one day, misery the next.

"No winter has passed so quietly and happily as this one," Andersen would write from the Nyhaven to Henriette Hanck. "*The Improvisatore* has procured me esteem from the most noble and best, even the mob has more respect, I have no anxiety for my daily bread, thank God, and lately I have been able to enjoy life thoroughly. The publishers send me newspapers, Reitzel books and prints; then I sit down wearing gay-colored slippers and a dressing-gown, with my feet on the sofa, the stove purrs, the tea-urn hums on the table, and the incense feels good. Then I think of the poor boy in Odense who wore wooden shoes, and my heart is soft and I bless the good God." And then it would be: "Oh God! What a creature I am! A soul-sick wretch. I often wish I had never been born or that I had not this erratic turn that makes me so unhappy."

Just as most people do not have transports of happiness that make them throw their arms round trees and kiss them, so they do not know this black melancholy. A poet has to learn that he is in the grip of his own moods, paying as it were for his gift, almost to diagnose himself, and this is hard to do; Andersen must often have looked round on his equable, sensible friends, serene with that tough and cool serenity which seems to flourish in the North, and wished that he were they.

If he had had a wife it might have been easier, but how could he marry? The little affluence *The Improvisatore* had brought did not last; though the Tales brought in a steady sum, it was small as yet; at times Andersen did not know how to pay his rent or keep himself decently dressed, and before thinking of a wife he would need at least two thousand rigsdaler a year.

Edvard Collin had married a sparkling dark-eyed girl, another Henriette, and perhaps this made Andersen, though thinking of the hopelessness of marriage, look round again on the girls he knew and he began to watch a certain little Sophie. She was the daughter of his old friend Örsted; not long ago she had sat on Andersen's knee and plagued him for stories; now she, like Louise, had grown up over night and was so demure with him that he began to think she was noticing him too. But what was the good? "I used to think of laurels," he wrote bitterly. "Now I think about the breadfruit tree."

But one day as he sat brooding in his small room that he had thought so cosy, somebody knocked at the door. It was a stranger "with beautiful and amicable features," the Count Conrad Rentzau-Breitenburg, a member of the Ministry. He had read *The Improvisatore* and had been impressed with its descriptions. In any other country but Denmark a poor author would have been summoned to the Minister; here the Minister climbed the stairs to the author's room.

It was Andersen's old fairy-tale luck; as they talked, the Count looked round the room and saw how bare it was—in spite of the sofa, the stove, the dressing-gown, the books—and presently, gently, he asked Hans Andersen if there were anything he could do for him.

Besides grants to the Theater and schools, the stipends for traveling, Denmark sets aside a sum for pensions to be given to those writers, painters, and composers whose work is worth while, and who hold no State office; most of the important poets had pensions—Oehlenschläger, Ingemann, Heiberg. Andersen knew this, but though Hertz, his contemporary, had just been awarded one, most of the holders were far older men and well established; even with the success of *The Improvisatore* and, in a lesser degree of *O.T.*, with a third novel, *Only a Fiddler*, just published, Andersen could not say he was established—again he did not count the Tales. But though he felt his claims were slender, he nerved himself to ask the Minister for a little State support. His luck held; soon he heard he had been granted a pension of four hundred rigsdaler a year.

It was not much, but life in Copenhagen was simple and Andersen's way of living very cheap; it meant the end of forced writing, the beginning of the hope that he could marry. "I have a little breadfruit tree in my garden," he said. "I need no longer sing for crumbs." And

it was more than money. It was recognition. "Now you
cannot complain," said Örsted. "Now you know you are
appreciated. Your reputation is founded."

Even as uncertain a being as Hans Andersen began
to feel it. The summer before, he had paid a visit to
Sweden. He had taken the canal steamer that traveled
for six days on the Göta Canal from Göteborg to Stockholm. Fredrika Bremer, the best-known Swedish writer
of her time, was on board and he found her out. At first
she was a little stiff with this long stranger who presented
himself to her, as so many young writers had done, of-
fering her his book to read; Andersen, however, had a
way of getting his will, and Miss Bremer found herself
taking the book and, back in her cabin, reading it. When
she came on deck again, she was quite changed and this
time it was she who looked for Andersen. They became
lifelong friends.

Sweden was always kind to Andersen; when he made
a second visit, to Lund, the university town, students
came marching in hundreds to give him an ovation.
When he came out on the steps of the house where he
was staying, they swept off their blue caps and stood
bareheaded in front of him. One of them asked for
three cheers "for the Master" and then made a speech.
"When Europe speaks of the great poet H. C. Andersen," he said, "do not forget that it was the students of
Lund who first gave you the public tribute you deserve."

When Andersen went home and the old monotonous
criticism began again, when people said "Oh yes, the
Swedes made a fuss of him!" even these pinpricks could

not make him forget the sight of all those upturned young faces, upturned in homage to him.

There was another recognition in these years, one that meant more to Andersen than anyone could know; he met Meisling, his old rector, in the street. He had suffered more from this man than from anyone else in his life, been driven almost out of his mind by fear of him; now he looked down on a fat shabby little man with a red nose, whose breath was rank with drink. Andersen was on his way out to dine, groomed, with clean linen and a fashionable coat, hat and cane. As he looked at the grotesque figure of his old master, certain words must have rung on the air: "Your verse will end as waste paper . . . and you in a lunatic asylum."

Meisling trembled and held out his hand. "I must tell you," he stammered, "that I know how wrong I have been." He could hardly get the words out; they were unmistakably sincere. He knew he had been cruel and how much he was below his old pupil; if Hans Andersen would only forgive. . . . Andersen would not let him finish; he took the little man's hand and all he felt was gladness that the strange inexplicable hatred was gone, that and sorrow that his old tormentor should be so derelict.

Yes, Hans Christian Andersen was solidly founded— odd words for him, but, after all, he had grown used to other words that were at first as strange. He gave up his rooms by the Canal and moved into a good hotel opposite his loved Royal Theater; he bought dandified clothes, he went "elegantly to elegant dinners"; he was asked to

speak at Thorvaldsen's feast. Henriette Wulff teased
him by saying he was nothing but a fine gentleman now,
but he was still Hans Andersen, the poet, and these were
only outside things; even the new little breadfruit tree
was not everything. Often, even in these happy days, he
was dark and haunted, and he had still that unhappy
knack of upsetting his own hard-won reputation.

Though *O.T.* and his third novel, *Only a Fiddler*,
were not as successful as *The Improvisatore*, they had
been quite well received, but now Andersen felt he did
not want to be a novelist. He had always loved the
theater; it was in his bones and he could not leave it
alone; he had adapted plays from foreign books, like
The Bride of Lammermoor; he had written librettos
for opera. Now he decided he would write a play that
would bring him enough money for marriage.

The plot was not his own; it was from a French short
story about a mulatto who, after great struggles, marries
the white Countess he has always loved. It was in verse
and Andersen worked at it earnestly, but when the play
was sent in, Molbech refused it at once; Andersen, angry
and astonished, protested. It is an indication of his growing status that it was read again; this time it was accepted, but there was still to be disappointment. On the
day of the performance he could watch from his rooms
as the bills were posted at the Theater, count the people
coming to take tickets, and his excitement grew. Then
grave news flashed through the streets; the King was
dead. There was, of course, no performance; indeed, the
Theater was closed for two months.

"I never had any luck in the theater," Hans Andersen was often to say. "It was never fair to me." It was almost too fair.

At the end of court mourning *The Mulatto* was given its first performance with every seat sold, and the applause at the end frightened Andersen, it was so much more than anything he had hoped. The new King, Christian VIII, sent for him and people crowded round him. Andersen was so uplifted that he plunged at once into another dark verse play, *The Moorish Maid*.

He had not a doubt of it; because *The Mulatto* had been a commercial success—it remained in the repertory for ten years—the Directors of the Theater Royal decided to put *The Moorish Maid* on, but Heiberg's wife, Denmark's best actress, refused to act in it. "I wrote it for you," stormed Andersen. She still refused.

It was not easy to be Andersen's friend. By refusing, Johanne Luise Heiberg was tacitly telling him it was poor; but Andersen was only hurt and bewildered. He was never able to assess his own work and it seemed to him that all his friends had turned on him.

While he was smarting from this, Louise Collin's marriage was announced. Andersen had known that one day she must marry Mr. Lind, but it was hurtful. There was another happy couple for him to congratulate, to watch, to envy; another new little home to visit and go away from, back to his lonely rooms. "I have imagined so much and had so little," he was to say afterwards.

Over and over again, this theme of being left out, of

being different from anybody else, comes into his work; it is in *The Little Mermaid*, *The Little Match-Seller*, *The Ugly Duckling*. There is a small, hardly known story called *Heartbreak* which in its little way sums up this theme; a tanner's widow had a pug dog who died; the grandchildren made him a grave,

so beautiful that it must have been quite pleasant to lie in it; it was bordered with broken flowerpots, strewn with sand, and at its head a broken beer bottle was stuck upside down; it was so beautiful that all the boys and girls were invited to look at it, the only price of admission being one trouser button, a thing every boy would have and which he could give the little girls.

So all the children from their street, and from the back lane as well, came along and paid their buttons. There were lots of them who had to get on with only one brace that afternoon; never mind, they had seen the pug dog's grave, and it was well worth the expense.

But outside the tanyard, right against the gate, was a little ragged girl, standing so gracefully there, with the prettiest curls and delightfully clear blue eyes. She didn't say a word, and she didn't cry, but every time the gate opened she looked in as far as she could. She hadn't a button—she knew that—and so she was left standing sadly outside, standing there till the others had all had their look at the grave and had gone away. Then at last she sat down, held her small brown hands before her face, and burst into tears; she alone had not seen the dog's grave. That was heartbreak, as bitter for her as it may sometimes be for one who is grown up.

Now Andersen's own lonely heart drove him to travel again, away from all the happy couples, the cosy domestic life, further and further, far beyond where he had ever been.

For the rest of his life he was to take these journeys, constantly, year after year. Hans Andersen belongs not only to Denmark, but to the whole world. A look in the Album shows this; there are contributions from all nationalities, all ages; letters as intimate from aged Lord Palmerston as from the little Crown Prince Valdemar, whose letter, in big round writing, has a picture of a steamship on the top. The Album has bars of music from Liszt, Schumann, Weber; letters from Dickens, Mendelssohn, Wilkie Collins, Jenny Lind. There are portraits of Alfred de Vigny, Balzac, Victor Hugo, Dumas, George Sand, David d'Angers, and the good-looking Lamartine, all the wits of Paris; Rachel wrote in it: *"L'art c'est le vrai,"* "Art is truth," and there are notes and pictures from Heine and Schiller, and a part of the manuscript of *William Tell*. When Andersen visited the Schiller household, Schiller's sister-in-law took her scissors and cut a few lines out of the poem and gave them to Andersen, the inveterate souvenir-hunter; it was only after much hunting among the museums of Europe that the missing lines were found.

Andersen's fourth journey was longer and more adventurous than any he had taken; this time he traveled on the railways. He described them minutely in his travel book, *Poet's Bazaar*: ". . . as many of my readers will not have seen a railroad," he wrote—and he confessed that before he went on it, he had a feeling that he called "railway fever"—"I must say that the first sensation was as if a child's hand drew a little carriage. The speed increases imperceptibly . . . but the train glides on like a sledge over a level snowfield. You look out of the windows and discover you are careering away as with horses at full gallop; it goes still quicker, you seem to fly but there is no shaking, no suffocation, nothing of what you anticipated would be unpleasant. The train stops a minute and a waiter hands in a tray of refreshments through the window, roasted pigeons literally fly into one's mouth . . . and then we are off again; soon we are suddenly under a roof where the train stops. It is Leipzig; we have come seventy miles in three hours!"

With a grant of money sent him by the King, Andersen took a ship from Italy to Greece and then on to Turkey; though he had suffered terribly over the news that had reached him, while he traveled, of the failure of *The Moorish Maid*, he came back up the Danube, feeling renewed and determined to do some serious work, perhaps revive *Agnete*. He brought home with him the new book of travels, *Poet's Bazaar*, but more important were two smaller books that were published before he went away: *A Picture Book without Pictures* and a fourth collection of Tales, *The Wild Swan*, *The Daisy*, and *The Staunch Tin Soldier*.

A little of Hans Andersen is in all his Tales; in some of them as obviously as his unhappiness in *Heartbreak*, his sufferings in *The Ugly Duckling*, his ambition in

The Fir Tree, but in *The Staunch Tin Soldier* a quality shines out that might be called the soul of Andersen; a little fantastic, and so gay and crisp that one almost forgets the steadfastness that is the point of the whole story. It was staunchness that molded the one-legged tin soldier, at last, into a glowing tin heart, and steadfastness that was beginning to make the scattered, complex Andersen into one whole poet.

XVI

IN the summers of his middle years, Andersen would leave Copenhagen and stay at the great manor houses of the country, at Nysö with Baroness Stampe, at Lyk-kesholm, Glorup, Gisselfeld, Bregentved, Frijsenborg in Jutland, and many others; houses where once upon a time Anne Marie would have thought herself privileged to help with the washing, where Andersen the father had not been good enough to be the cobbler, and where now their son was welcomed as an honored guest.

"In the homes of what are called the greatest families of the country I met some kind, warm-hearted people, who appreciated the good in me and admitted me to their circles, let me participate in their happiness in their rich summer life; independent, I could there quite sur-render to nature, to the solitude of the woods, and to the life in a manor house; there, for the first time, I lived with Danish nature, there I wrote most of my Tales. In this world of quiet lakes in the woods, and the green grass fields where the game . . . roebuck, pheas-ants . . . leapt across, and the stork sauntered on his red legs, I didn't hear any politics or polemics, did not hear anybody talk according to Hegel; nature around me and within me preached my mission to me."

These manors were like whole villages, spreading in farms and workshops over two or three acres, the manor house itself rising in gables and turrets, or else flat-fronted like the beautiful Glorup, which looks like a château with its copper-domed cupola, its scrolled iron gates, its fountains and statues standing among the trees in the beech groves. The trees under which Andersen walked and dreamed still stand there and the country stretches quietly away on all sides. Fyn is called the garden of Denmark, and the green, the rich crops, the roses and clover were to Andersen like a garden in Eden.

These idle counts and baronesses left Andersen in quiet to write. "I can walk for hours in silent contemplation, but I hope those hours are not wasted; they work as the rays of the sun on the negative of the daguerreotype, the true picture is absorbed and stays there. . . ."

Picture after picture; book by book, more Tales came out, *The Ugly Duckling*, *The Top and the Ball*, *The Little Fir Tree*, *The Snow Queen*, *The Snow Man*, *The Ice Maiden*, *The Rose Elf*. All together there are one hundred and sixty-eight Tales, of which one hundred and fifty-six were printed in Andersen's own time.

But still, obstinately, with all his success, he hankered after the theater and in 1844 he wrote a little play, *The Lying-in Room*, which he decided to offer anonymously. "If they don't know it is Andersen they will accept it," he said bitterly. As if to prove him right, it was taken and produced quite successfully, and was to stay in the repertoire until 1942. He was more than ever convinced that there was nothing between him and the theater but prejudice. It seems extraordinary that he could not have been content, but perhaps in everyone there is this voice crying for the moon.

Each year brought him more fame; soon, as well as manor houses, he stayed in palaces. He went to Weimar to pay reverence to the place where Goethe had lived, and there he met the handsome blue-eyed young man who was Carl Alexander, the Hereditary Grand Duke of Weimar; from the first moment they were friends. The Duke and his young Duchess taught Andersen some things about royalty that he had not dreamed of and that perhaps helped him to make his own princes and queens so human; he must have smiled when he remembered the stilted made-up language he had once invented for them. The Grand Duchess picnicked with her children in the woods, and they, the little Prince Carl August, and his brothers and sisters gathered round Andersen clamoring for stories as if they were little Drewsens or Collins, or his own landlady's daughter at home. Almost every year Andersen paid a visit to Weimar, and letters went backwards and forwards.

The King of Prussia invited him to court, and he visited his own King and Queen of Denmark while the court was at a summer bathing place. He sat at the King's table, that very King Christian with whom, as Prince Governor, he had once been given the audience in Odense; had the King forgotten, Andersen wondered, that advice to become a turner?

He was naïvely happy in these royal friendships. "After all," he makes the nightingale say of the Emperor, "there is something holy about a crown"; but his friends, especially the Collins, did not understand it; it seemed to them snobbish and extravagant and what had always repelled the sensible practical Collin family was Hans Christian's extravagance. It never occurred to them that what would have been extravagant for them, or for Hans Christian the foundling, was not extrava- gant for Hans Andersen. People are different sizes, thank God, but never, to the end of their lives, did the Collins know Andersen's size. Now they smiled at his letters from this court or that, and they did not, in fact, quite believe them until a young Collin was taken by Andersen to visit Weimar and saw for himself how the family protégé was received. There is a little word that irresistibly comes to mind for the Collins; for all their faithfulness, they were smug; it made them limited, and Andersen, though he was their devoted brother as long as he lived, had outgrown them, for he was reaching his full stature.

Once upon a time he might have gone to people's houses as an exhibitionist, to amuse them, one might almost say with his antics, but now he went as an equal. His studies, his travels, his constant meetings with gifted, cultured men and women, had mellowed him; he was no longer crude and raw.

Even his looks had altered. His ugliness had weath- ered into a dignity and nobility that was striking. He no longer winced at remarks about his length and bigness. "Look, my galoshes have had children!" he said once, seeing his immense pair among the Collin family ones. He was sought after, not only because of his Tales, but for himself. He seemed integrated, whole, but in him there was still the dissatisfied restless longing.

These languorous poetical days in the old manors and palaces, the beauty, the picnics and music, the bare shoulders and laces, the diamonds sparkling in scented hair, had wakened him again; as in the old garden at the Iversens' and in those warm Neapolitan nights, he quivered with feeling; after all he was not forty and had the strength of the untried. "What do I live for?" he sometimes asked. "Am I not a man?" It seems fitting that at this moment, in a small party of Bournonville's, the master of the Royal Ballet, Andersen should meet a shy, serious young woman, whose face seemed plain until she spoke; then, startlingly, she was almost beautiful.

"Watch a woman who can be beautiful and ugly," says the proverb, "she is rare." Very often that evening Hans Andersen found himself watching this one. She sang, and after it he was so strangely moved that he could no longer stay in the room. A few nights later he heard her at the Theater Royal, when she sang Alice in *Robert of Normandy*; the staid Copenhagen audience rose to its feet and gave the small figure, bowing in the glare of light in front of the curtain, such an ovation that Andersen, standing among them, was giddy and deaf. He seemed to have a tumult in his ears, in his brain, in his heart. That night at Bournonville's, his toast was drunk with hers in champagne and he knew he was in love—not in love again—this was something utterly new and fresh.

The girls he had loved till now, Riborg, Louise,

Sophie, had been good ordinary Danish daughters, brought up to be housewives. This new "she" was like no one he had known; she was herself, unique, a revelation; though she was only twenty-three, her knowledge and wisdom were extraordinary; they seemed to come from the same natural fountain as her singing, which was really like an enchanted bird's. Denmark called her the Swedish Nightingale; her real name was Jenny Lind.

Instinctively one thinks of her as little and brown, perhaps because she was so often called a nightingale, perhaps because Hans Andersen wrote of her as that little brown bird in *The Emperor's Nightingale*; in reality she was tall, slender, and graceful. In Andersen's Album there is a picture of her wearing a low dress and deep lace collar; her hair—it was auburn—falls in such a galaxy of ringlets that they look topheavy each side of a wide forehead that is a little heavy too; but the whole head is poised with singular grace on a very long neck. People have said that her gray eyes changed remarkably as she sang.

Her career was extraordinary in that it had no reverses, the opposite of Andersen's. It was a steady mounting triumph; her audiences were not only captivated but overcome by an emotion that seems to have been indescribable, though plenty of them tried to describe it.

It began when, as a child, she used to sit in the window of her grandmother's apartment in Stockholm and sing to the cat, and the people passing in the street stopped to hear and wonder; among them was the maid of one of the dancers at the Royal Opera House. "You talk of your opera singers," the maid told her mistress. "You ought to hear that little girl with the cat."

The dancer heard her and at once sent her to the Director of Singing.

From that day the Royal Opera House at Stockholm took charge of Jenny Lind; it kept, educated, and trained her and finally sent her abroad, where, as every-one knows, Copenhagen, Berlin, Paris, Milan, London, New York, one after another, went mad over her.

She and Andersen were good companions. Once, on one of their walks in Copenhagen, feeling hungry, they went into a baker's shop and ate hot buns and milk. The baker recognized them and refused to be paid, saying he was honored enough by a visit from two such celebrities, but Jenny paid him. Standing in the little shop by the counter, she sang one of her famous folk songs for him, and then she and Andersen went on for their walk.

From the beginning Andersen knew he had very lit-tle hope. As she boarded the ship that was to take her away that first time, he put a letter in her hand, "a letter that she must understand." She understood it so well that she thought it better not to answer it. A year or two afterwards he tried again; when they were staying in the country he carefully separated her from the others on a walk, meaning to propose, but before he could speak she had said briskly: "Come along, Andersen, don't let's get left behind," and she ran on.

In December of 1845 he went to Berlin, where she was singing, hoping to spend Christmas with her, but though she knew he was there she did not send for him. He sat alone in his hotel room and wrote miserably in his diary: "I wonder what fills her thoughts . . . she takes so little notice of me, who came to Berlin chiefly for her sake. It is Christmas Eve. How happy the home is where the husband has a hearth! The Christmas tree is lighted; his wife stands with the youngest in her arms . . . it stretches its hands towards the lights; the other children are jubilant . . ." but it was no use dreaming. When at last she did send for him and they spent New Year's Eve together, he knew it was no use. For the first time they were quite alone; even Jenny's companion was not there. She lighted the Christmas tree for Andersen and with her lovely voice sang peace and happiness into his soul, but she made it quite clear that she could give him nothing else.

He has told a little of what she meant to him in *The Emperor's Nightingale*. He wrote many fairy tales for Jenny Lind, *The Angel*, *The Willow*, but none like this, as sure, as balanced, as telling, or as poignant. It begins very simply, a beginning that is often quoted as one of the most perfect in all literature: "In China, you know, the Emperor is Chinese, and all the people are Chinese . . ." and goes on to tell of the nightingale who sang in the wood and how the Emperor learned to prize his free little brown bird, with the throbbing living song in its throat, more than the glittering jeweled one with its clever musical box. "I can't make my home in the palace," said the nightingale, "but let me come when I want to; then I'll sing of an evening on this branch by the window, and my singing can make you both gay and thoughtful. I shall sing of those that are happy, and of those that suffer; I shall sing of the good and the evil that are here lurking about you."

Andersen saw Jenny Lind many times again, but she married Otto Goldschmidt, the pianist; by that time Andersen had quietly accepted that he was to be alone.

XVII

IT was in the summer of 1847 that Andersen traveled in a new direction, to England.

"London is the city of cities," he wrote. "Here is Paris but with a mightier power; here is the life of Naples but without its bustle." Not bustle but Bedlam: he was terrified of the traffic. "Omnibus after omnibus passes—they say there are four thousand—teams, carts, cabs, hansoms, and elegant carriages are rattling, training, rolling, and driving away. . . . Where the streets cross one another there is an elevated place, where people rush from the sidewalks through the nearest line of carriages, waiting in that asylum for a chance to get through the other line and on to the opposite sidewalk." He found it terribly tiring; it was hot, as only London can be hot; Copenhagen, built on the sea, is a fresh clean city; Andersen was appalled at the dirt of London, especially what he called "the coal-smoke air."

He had brought no letters of introduction, but the Danish Ambassador, Count Reventlow, on whom he called the first morning, told him he did not need any; "Everybody knows you," said the Count.

That seemed true; the first night Andersen was asked to a party at Lord Palmerston's and, from that moment, he was heaped with invitations. "Tonight you have made a jump into high life which most of us take years to come into," said Count Reventlow.

There were great names enough, even for Andersen. He talked to the Duchess of Suffolk, the Duke of Cambridge; it is interesting to know from his diary that he was introduced to a lady whom he describes as Jane Austen's daughter (she was Lady Duff-Gordon); he met a deaf lady with a long ear-trumpet at a garden party; she wrote "political things," and after talking to her he had to lie down the whole afternoon; it was the redoubtable Miss Martineau.

The season was in full swing and Andersen was invited out every day for dinner, or for the evening, and after that to balls; he was even obliged to go out to breakfast, a common thing in England then, and there was a crowd everywhere he went. "It was just one long day and night," he wrote, and he could not stand it.

The English and American ways of life always seem costly and complicated to the Danes; they certainly seemed so to simple Hans Andersen. He had arranged to stay at a quiet little hotel, the Hotel de Sablonière in Leicester Square, but that appalled Count Reventlow; it was not nearly fashionable enough. "Stay there if you must," he told Andersen, "but for Heaven's sake say you are staying at the Embassy." "In this land of freedom, one almost dies of etiquette," groaned Andersen. "Even the Queen, wanting to stay out in the park one glorious summer evening, was obliged to go home because the palace dinner must be at eight o'clock, eight o'clock precisely."

But he liked the ordinary people; just as we talk of the politeness of the Danes, he talked of the politeness of the English, especially the policemen; but the enormous contrast between rich and poor horrified him.

He had never seen so many famished men and women. "They glide by like shadows," he wrote home, "and place themselves in front of a person and gaze at him with hungry sad expressions on their pale pinched faces." They were not allowed to ask for alms and carried a piece of pasteboard round their necks with "Mercy. I am starving," written on it. At the same time he had never seen such elaborate dresses and houses. "Almost everywhere the principal figures are the same," he wrote, "only varying in gold, satin, lace, and flowers." With his perpetual interest in flowers he particularly noticed how often roses were used in the decoration of the rooms; windows, tables, staircases, and niches were covered with roses. He satisfied himself that they were always placed in water, though vases could not be seen; to the eye, the roses formed entire carpets, fragrant and fresh. The longing for fragrance and freshness overpowered him and he escaped to see Jenny Lind.

"The topic of the day in London was Jenny and only Jenny," he wrote. In an attempt to achieve privacy she had hired a house in Old Brompton; he found out on the map where that was and went in an omnibus; the conductor told him how far he was to go and where he should find the house of "the Swedish Nightingale."

It was a little house, with a low hedge shutting out the street. People were standing outside trying to get a glimpse of Jenny Lind, and that day they had a chance; she recognized Andersen from the windows, and ran out and shook both his hands, forgetting the crowd. "We hastened into the house, which was pretty and rich," wrote Andersen. "Elegantly bound books lay on the table. She showed me my own *True Story of My Life*, which Mary Howitt had dedicated to her; a large sheet lay on the table, it was a caricature of Jenny Lind, a great nightingale with a girlish face; Lumley, the impresario, was shown putting sovereigns on her tail to get her to sing." They talked of home, of Bournonville and Collin. When she saw how exhausted and tired Andersen was, she said: "Now you know what it is like to be at a perpetual feast," and she was silent and sighed.

It was not many years later that, at the height of her fame, in full career, still young, promising even more to come, Jenny Lind suddenly retired. No one could understand why, it seemed madness, but Andersen, who loved her, had almost predicted that sigh in the garden at Old Brompton, and in *The Emperor's Nightingale* he had written of how the marvelous little bird, after her triumph, was sentenced to "remain at court and have her own cage, with leave to go out for two walks in the daytime and one at night. She was given twelve attendants who each held on tightly to silk ribbon fastened round her leg. There was absolutely no fun in a walk like that."

Jenny had always had a profound effect on Andersen. After being with her he was able to single out what was valuable and true in the lavishness and glitter, and remember what it was that he had come to England to do.

For years he had wanted to meet Dickens and for this he went to Lady Blessington at Gore House. "Don't tell anyone you are going there," said Count Reventlow. "At least, don't tell the ladies." Andersen quite serenely told everyone.

This was near the time of Lady Blessington's final defeat, bankruptcy, withdrawal to France, and death. For years she had fought a brilliant battle against scandal, overwork, and debt from extravagance, the last not as much her own as from the fabulous spendings of the Count d'Orsay, husband of her stepdaughter and in whom most of the scandal centered.

Andersen had heard of the parties to which no women were invited but where gifted men from all over Europe, even from America, came for such talk and food as could not be found anywhere else in London. Lady Blessington understood the value of background; Andersen was awed by the crimson and gold drawing-room, the green library, and the intimate dining-room where the hostess sat at the head of the table in what was almost a chair of state; she wore one of the plain, low-cut gowns of dark satin or velvet that set off the beauty of her arms and neck. The end was not far off, but Lady Blessington is famous for a saying: "There are few with whom one can condescend to seem otherwise than happy," and Andersen saw only the splendor, the charm and understanding that had made her the close friend of so many gifted men, even such a difficult genius as Byron.

Dickens was there, youthful and handsome, with a

kind, wise expression and long, beautiful hair. "We shook hands," said Andersen, "looked into each other's eyes, and when we spoke, we understood."

The other dream was to go to Scotland, which for Andersen was only one thing, "Walter Scott's country." Long ago he had gone without his dinner to get pennies to pay the library fees on Scott's novels; now, touring the Highlands, he found his name nearly as well known as his hero's. He lost his walking-stick at Loch Lomond, and at Edinburgh, as he was boarding the London train on his way back, the conductor came running up to him with the lost stick; it had traveled all over the Highlands to find him and its only label was "The Danish poet, Hans Andersen."

"My portrait hangs next to Jenny Lind's in the shops," he wrote to King Christian, and, to the Grand Duke of Weimar: "My stay in England and Scotland floats before me like a fantasy of joy and sunshine."

It ended with a visit to Dickens at Broadstairs, and the last person he saw on English shores was Dickens, who surprised him by coming to Ramsgate to go on board the boat with him and, when the ship started, stood on the very edge of the quay, looking sturdy, youthful, and handsome, and waving his hat.

For Hans Andersen, the English author was too haloed with admiration and sentiment to have any faults, but that Dickens criticized his Danish friend was shown only too plainly when Andersen came back to England to stay at Gadshill ten years later.

He was not an easy guest. To begin with he was that

hostess's dread, the guest who can never be left alone; fortunately the children did not mind being pressed into service; "and we have plenty of those," said Dickens, all those little boys with literary names, Walter Landor, Edward Bulwer-Lytton, Henry Fielding, Sydney Smith, Alfred Tennyson. Then he was so ridiculously sensitive. Mrs. Dickens found him one day, sobbing full-length in the grass, a newspaper clutched in one hand. "Is one of your friends dead?" she asked, but it was a review, "a perfectly nasty review," of one of his novels in a newspaper. There was also the difficulty of the language; he could not learn to speak English and he took fright so easily. Once in London, they sent him in a cab by himself and, not understanding the driver, he thought he was being driven away with. Dickens made a tall story of it, telling how Andersen stuffed his watch, his studs, and his money down his boots. The Dickens girls said he was a "boney bore," and in the end it was only kind Mrs. Dickens—so like Agnes in *David Copperfield*—who of the grownups cared for him.

When he had gone, Dickens stuck a card up on the dressing-table mirror: "Hans Andersen slept in this room for five weeks; it seemed to the family ages."

Andersen was quite unaware of this; though he did write: "I always had the fear that you would get tired of me, the stranger who could not speak your tongue," the time seemed to him idyllic. "The whole landscape is like a garden," he wrote home, "and from the hills one can follow the winding Thames for many a mile

and, looking far over woods and fields, catch a glimpse
of the sea." The large field of clover close to the house
made a good playground. "The sons and I are often
lying there," wrote Hans Andersen, "there is a fragrance of clover, the elder tree is in blossom, and the
wild roses have an odor of apples so fresh and strong."
He basked in the family life and saw no sign of any rift
between his host and hostess; both personified to him
"the spirit of true amiability," and, less critical and
egotistical than his English contemporary—whose lack
of loyalty to his guest and friend makes us ashamed for
him—Andersen confidently kept his dear Boz on his
long and growing list of famous friends, and one of his
letters was carefully pasted into a place of honor in the
Album.

But Andersen was not as confident of his friends at
home and he had some reason to think his own country
was not fair to him. The Danish press had unaccountably
refused to publish any of the articles or pictures that appeared about him abroad, and when he had come back
from England, that first time, he heard someone say,
pointing him out in the street: "Look, our orang-outang,
who is so famous abroad, is back!"

It had been going on for a long time; in 1845 his
friend Hauch, led by some obscure jealousy and spite,
had pilloried him in a novel, *The Castle on the Rhine.*
In the book there was a poet so fantastically vain that he
rushed up and introduced himself to people, read aloud
relentlessly, made parents bring their children forward so
that he could tell them stories; the poet was shown as a

physical coward who wept at criticism, and traveled
abroad to get appreciation; in the end he went mad, and
when the jeering riffraff put him in a cart and dragged
him off to the madhouse, he still proudly believed they
were honoring him as the greatest poet in the world.

It was a cruel portrait; much of it was true and it
was glaringly public. "People in Copenhagen keep asking me: 'What have you done to Hauch?'" Andersen
wrote to Ingemann. "And I have answered that Hauch
never had me in mind, that he has a noble and magnani-
mous disposition and bears friendship and kindness to
me." But Andersen had not then read the book; all
Copenhagen waited to see what would happen when he
did. They expected an outcry, but they saw something
they had seen before, Andersen turning the tables, as
he had long ago in a drawing-room when he was asked
to read aloud as a joke.

He sent another letter to Ingemann, so full of dignity
that Ingeman felt obliged to go to Hauch with it.

Copenhagen, Sept. 16, 1845

*Just after I had sent my last letter from Bregentved
I got Hauch's novel; I must judge people otherwise now
I've seen this figure [of the poet]; they are right to say
"It is Andersen!" Here all my weaknesses are collected!
I think and hope that I have lived through this period;
but everything that this poet says and does, I might have
said and done; I felt shockingly impressed by this crude
portrait, which showed me in my misery. Still, I believe
that in order to depict me truly it needs a considerable
supplement, which, I trust, would contain a good many*

*better elements, through which I should become more
tolerable in life, I might almost say "less contemptible":
I'm perfectly convinced, though, that Hauch has not
meant there to be such a great similarity as there really
is, it has not occurred to him that everybody was com-
pelled to pin it on me. I know he appreciates the good
that is in me; I have the greatest confidence in him and
affection for him still and will keep it. What has shocked
me, what scorches my thought now and then, is the end
of the miserable poet. My own grandfather was insane,
my father's mind was affected shortly before his death.
There is nothing to do, nothing to say; it is a breaker I
have to let wash over me; the most bitter part of it is
that I, being a little more sensible than my caricature,
must try hereafter to be a little less open; but that is said
to be good and prudent. Remember me cordially to
Hauch.*

*Affectionately yours,
H. C. Andersen*

No wonder that Hauch felt thoroughly small and mean.

The effect of his own large-mindedness stayed with
Andersen down the years; criticism pained him as much
as ever but, except for occasional outbursts of tears like
that at Gadshill, he was able to meet it with dignity; he
had, what all great and lovable people have, humility;
it is only those who are unsure of themselves who need
to be conceited, and if, on the second English visit,
Dickens had sometimes appeared to avoid his guest, not
to want to walk with him arm in arm through those

streets of London that he had made so real, Andersen
shut his eyes to it. He knew he was tiresome and knew,
equally well, that in spite of it, he was loved.

There was one love that was new to him; he, who
had adored so many young girls was now adored and,
more surprisingly still, by a Collin, Jonna Drewsen,
Ingeborg's daughter; she had been a pale, thin leggy
little girl with large dark eyes that always seemed fixed
on Andersen's face when he went to the Drewsens'; at
first he thought of it as a child's love, but she grew up,
with the same swiftness that had surprised him in her
Aunt Louise and Sophie Örsted, into a dark girl, not
very tall, with an imperious little mouth and level
brows. In a moment, it seemed, she was someone to
whom he should no longer say "thou," but Jonna passionately insisted on being called "thou" "as long as you
care for me," to which Andersen answered: "Then as
long as life shall last."

It was a strange last gift for him but he loved Jonna
enough to encourage her to marry someone else; she had
a secret romance with Henrik Stampe, the son of Andersen's old friend the Baroness of Nysö.

The young Baron saw Jonna first in the box that Collin, as a Director, had at the Theater. It was Andersen
who introduced them, who carried their letters and persuaded the Baroness to give her consent, where she had
harshly disapproved, and he put all three of them into
The Shepherdess and the Chimney Sweep. Perhaps
when Andersen was alone, thinking of the two young
lovers, at last together, a chimney sweep had come in to

mend the chimney, one of the Danish sweeps who wear a tall top hat; or perhaps it was the porcelain works that are the fame of Copenhagen, with their exquisitely modeled and colored figures, that put it into his mind.

Jonna is the little china shepherdess. ". . . She wore golden shoes and looped up her gown fetchingly with a red rose. Her hat was gold, even her crook was gold. She was simply charming." Young Henrik was the chimney sweep and, because Andersen did not like to make even such a near friend who was a Baron into a chimney sweep, the story tells that he was made of the finest porcelain. ". . . He was as clean and tidy as anyone could be because, you see, he was only an ornamental chimney sweep. If the china-makers had wanted to, they could just as easily have turned him out as a prince, for he had a jaunty way of holding his ladder and his cheeks were as pink as a girl's. That was a mistake, don't you think? His shoulders should have been daubed with a pinch or two of soot. . . . The chimney sweep and the shepherdess stood close together on a table and they became engaged because they suited each other exactly, but near them stood another figure, three times as big as they . . . an old Chinaman who could nod his head." This was the Baroness, and it is to be hoped she did not recognize herself.

Jonna was, for Andersen, a little piece of intelligence and idealism in years when the world seemed strangely full of stupidity and ugliness. Thorvaldsen had died and Oehlenschläger, and twice in a decade Denmark was at war with Prussia, causing Andersen to suffer the peculiar

torments of someone who has dear friends on both sides.
The King of Prussia had honored him, sent him the
Order of the Red Eagle; it was publicly known that
Hans Andersen was an admirer of Germany. He was
called unpatriotic, which hurt him, but how could he,
who had made himself international, have the blind
patriotism of those who knew only Denmark? Hate the
Germans? He thought they were wickedly, disastrously
wrong, but he could not hate men in whose houses he
had been a cherished guest, women with whom he had
sat and talked, children to whom he had told his Tales.
"You don't find me fervent enough in my Danishness,
dear Jonna," he wrote, for Jonna, even Jonna, had joined
in. "Perhaps it arises from the fact that I am 'just' to
everybody. Is that a crime?"

Though he refused to enter the bitter partisanship,
his heart was torn for his little country. Almost every
day troops of young men marched off and he wrote the
song *I cannot stay, I have no rest,* for them; it became
a popular war song; more important, all his love and
feelings were poured into the *Hymn for Denmark,*
which is the epigraph of this book: "In Denmark was I
born, and there 'tis homely. . . ."

Homely even in the midst of war. In a letter from
the front, one of his friends told him how, in a town
where all the houses were shattered and riddled with
cannon balls and grapeshot, on one house was a stork's
nest, holding a new stork family. It seemed to Andersen
a symbol of a vast pattern that he had glimpsed before.
On the day of King Christian VIII's death, just before

the war, a wild swan had flown against the spire of Roskilde Cathedral, where all the kings and queens of Denmark lie in their coffins; the swan bruised its breast but was able to fly again. In one of the wreaths on Oehlenschläger's tomb a songbird was found to have built its nest; once Andersen had written with his cane in the snow: "Immortality is like snow, tomorrow sees no trace"; he had gone away, there had been a thaw, and, coming to the place again, he had found that all the snow had melted except for one little spot where remained the word "immortality." The storks made him hope again that peace and happiness would come back to Denmark.

XVIII

O Danish tongue, your tones are soft and comely,
None but a mother's tongue could soothe like
those . . .

but if his country could soothe Andersen, she could
scold as well. Denmark was still a stern mother, but
she knew what was best for him; as the years went by
she seemed to identify him more and more with his
Tales. The novels and travel books, though they had
several editions, faded slowly into the background; some
of his poems are to be found in every anthology, but
most are forgotten; though his opera *Liden Kirsten* is
often staged, the plays have kept only their moderate
places in time.

Andersen still agonized over this. A rival theater
to the Royal opened in Copenhagen now; it had been
started by the man who was to lay out the Tivoli pleasure gardens and who was glad to take any sort of play
from a well-known writer, but though several of Andersen's plays were produced there, Andersen knew it had
not the standard of the Royal Theater, whose directors,
he swore, were unfair. "They spit on me when all Europe has honored me," he said.

It was he who was unfair; again and again they had
tried him; they had put on his student play and *The
Mulatto, The Moorish Maid, Agnete*; even today the

costumes of his *Twelve Months,* carefully kept, can be seen hanging up in the vast wardrobe rooms of the new Royal Theater; it was not the directors' fault, but the fault of the plays, that they failed. "That confounded theater!" said Edvard. "It is only it that comes between you and Denmark. Is it, then, the whole of Denmark? Are you not something more than a playwright? Is it as such that you are made so much of in Germany, for instance?"

Andersen knew very well it was not and slowly he began to see that Edvard was right. Though his novel *The Four Baronesses,* his travel book on Spain, and the long epic about the Wandering Jew were all written in his later years, he began to accept the verdict and let his life work be the Tales.

He could not help it; they had taken full charge of him. The defeat of 1864, when Denmark had to yield Schleswig-Holstein to the Prussians, was bitter for any Dane, but the Tales were in the German nurseries as well as in the Danish ones; they were there when the battle began and when it ended; wars and disputes had nothing to do with them, for they were universal. The children of England and America had them, the children of France; there was even a translation into Hindustani.

There had been an illustrated edition in Germany; now Andersen was asked to look for an illustrator for Denmark. He chose a young naval officer, Vilhelm Pedersen, whose delicate drawings have become classic to Danish readers; they may now be thought a little indefinite and old-fashioned, but they are the traditional illustrations for Andersen's Tales, just as Tenniel is traditional for *Alice in Wonderland*. There have been shockingly bad illustrations, from Mabel Lucie Atwell's grotesque dumps of elves to ornamental wishy-washy whimsies like Margaret Tarrant's, but Lorenz Frölich, a Dane, illustrated the later Tales very finely, and another Dane, the painter Syberg, did an edition of *The Story of a Mother* from which two murals were taken for the entrance hall of the Museum at Odense. There was also Hans Tagner, and in later years Fritz Kredel, who illustrated the Hersholt edition; but Pedersen, to the Danes, is the right illustrator, and his drawings are in the small books of the Keigwin translations.

Already in Andersen's lifetime people spoke of traditional drawings, and first editions were rare; they had been read and handled by so many children that most had fallen to pieces. In Paris, on the Quai d'Orsay, Andersen was asked double the original price for a tattered edition of *A Picture Book without Pictures*, and the bookseller was overwhelmed when told who his customer was.

At the end of *The Ugly Duckling* comes that description of how the clumsy, ugly, grayish bird is recognized as a swan:

> He felt positively glad at having been through so much hardship and want; it helped him to appreciate all the happiness and beauty that were there to welcome him . . . and the great swans swam round and round and stroked him with their beaks.

Some little children came into the garden and threw bread and grain into the water and the smallest one cried out: "There's a new swan!". . . and they clapped their hands with delight and danced about and ran to fetch their father and mother. Bits of bread and cake were thrown into the water and everyone said: "The new one is the prettiest" and the old swans bowed before him.

This made him feel quite shy and he tucked his head away under his wing . . . he was too, too happy but not a bit proud, for a good heart is never proud . . . and the lilacs bowed their branches to him right down into the water and the sunshine felt so warm and kindly. Then he ruffled his feathers on his neck and rejoiced from his heart. "I never dreamed of such happiness when I was the ugly duckling."

Andersen had ease and comfort now. His pension was raised. He had not asked for it; indeed, years before, when King Christian had questioned him about his finances, he had said quite contentedly that he had a State pension of four hundred rigsdaler a year. "But how little!" said the King.

"I earn something with my pen," Andersen reminded him.

The King had said firmly: "You ought to be more comfortable than that," but Andersen had insisted it was enough. His friends at court had thought him ridiculous. "The King was actually *asking* you to ask for more," they said, but Andersen had only laughed and said he had had enough of begging in his early days.

The pension was raised now as a tribute and later he was given the title of Professor.

His life now seems like a kaleidoscope; the pictures come and go so quickly, repeating themselves in a medley of time and place, that it is hardly possible to separate the years. There were the brilliant friendships; King Christian had died, but Andersen found a new friend in Frederik VII, who sent him a gold box set with diamonds and sometimes invited him to court. Andersen had become a polished courtier; once, at table, Frederik raised his glass to him. The Danes are sensitive about this custom of drinking healths; the host drinks to each guest, the guests drink to him and to each other with real ceremony. The King drank to Andersen, but Andersen had nothing but water in his glass; hoping the green color of the goblet would hide this, he raised it in return, but the King said jokingly: "When you drink with your King, you drink wine." Andersen parried this at once. "When I drink with my King, water is made wine," he said.

Probably no other writer was honored in his life as was Andersen; he had craved for fame, he was given it, brimming over. When he visited Portugal, the Danish ships ran up their flags for him in Lisbon harbor, and young Jonas Collin, traveling with him, was disgusted and disconcerted at the ovations they met with everywhere they went.

There were dark days of mourning; Andersen and Jonas were in Lucerne together when word came that

old Counselor Collin was dying; they reached Copenhagen in time for the funeral. Years ago Andersen had
been summoned in the night because Mrs. Collin was
sinking "and the children were gathering." To be in-
cluded, at such a moment, as one of them had touched
and gratified him deeply and he never forgot it; it was
as a son that he looked down on the calm kind face of
his benefactor in the coffin and as a son he mourned.

These were years of loss; Ingemann died and Andersen went to Sorö to be with his widow. Orsted died, but
worst of all had been the death of Henriette Wulff in
1858 on her way to America when the steamship
Austria caught fire in mid-Atlantic and sank. Andersen
wrote about it in his diary: "From England came her
last letter to her sister; she had said she felt some repug-
nance for the journey—which was odd in one who
loved the sea so passionately and had crossed to America
before—that she had almost turned back but shamed
herself out of her weakness and went on." There were
descriptions of the fearful scenes by the few who were
saved, but she, with her little feeble form, was not among
them; she had been seen to go to her stateroom and it
was thought she had been suffocated by the smoke and
died there.

The news tortured Andersen; he mourned for his
little gay weak friend and ever afterwards, for fear of
fire, he carried a rope with him when he traveled; it can
be seen with his luggage at Odense. Henriette's death,
too, made him even more afraid of the sea.

For a long time letters had been coming across the

Atlantic, letters of praise and thanks, many of them invitations to come to America. Dickens had gone to America, and Jenny Lind; Henriette Wulff herself had always urged Andersen to come. "There is the vast ocean between us," he had written in answer to one of her letters, "fourteen days of broad angry sea where I should for days be seasick in return for my money out of pocket." The money was another thing. "Do you know how you might allure me?" he had told her. "Why, by writing so much for the steamer, so much a day in a good hotel, so much per mile by rail." Once he said he might go if a rich man or woman over there left him the money in a will, but he retracted that. He was frightened too of America itself: "I should not know how to make even a fairy behave herself with propriety there," he said.

He never went. Henriette's death had shaken him and he felt that, with his travels and eminent circles, he had neglected his old friends; now their ranks were thinned, they seemed to be dearer than ever and he clung to them. He took Collin grandchildren with him on his travels, Viggo Drewsen, who was Ingeborg's son and Jonna's brother, or else young Jonas, the son of Edvard; nothing in his life gave him more pleasure than to benefit these young men, to give back some little part of all he had been given.

Viggo, in his photograph, has a delightful piquant face, but Jonas, with his tight lips, small eyes, and his entire preoccupation with his zoology—he is even photographed with an animal skeleton—seems to have been a prig, with little of Edvard's humanity. On the travels Jonas continually criticized and reproved Andersen, who bore it patiently; he knew that nothing young Jonas could say or do could prevent Andersen's greatness; tides of it even began to roll home and soon this lanky writer, whom no one could possibly mistake, was a national hero.

The Queen Dowager asked him to stay with her in her palace; another new King, Christian IX—Andersen lived through four reigns—made him a State Counselor, the very title old Collin, Jonas's grandfather, had had.

Then, on the 6th of December 1867, Hans Andersen was invited to Odense to be given the freedom of the city, to stay at the Bishop's house for the ceremony and the banquet, the public holiday, the children's singing, and the illuminations. "He will be a wild high-flying bird and one day all Odense will be illuminated for him," the wisewoman had said. It had come full circle.

XIX

AT sixty-two Andersen was a tired and nervous old man;
his hard life, the poverty and underfeeding he had en-
dured as a boy, the tension at which he lived, had worn
him out.

His nerves were a torment; there was the fear of the
sea; to cross the Great Belt was an agony and another
visit to England out of the question, though he had
been invited to the marriage of the Prince of Wales
to the beautiful Princess Alexandra of Denmark. There
was the fear of fire; his terror of having left candles
alight made him go again and again to look into any
room he had left. There were fears of death; perhaps
because there was an outbreak of cholera in the city or,
equally, because a mosquito had bitten him. Things
were always conspiring to bite him. *"Did* that dog bite
me?" he once asked his landlady. There were fears of
missing trains; on his travels he nearly drove young
Jonas frantic by insisting on getting to the station hours
before the train started.

He still traveled with his rope, the battered valises,
and sometimes with young Jonas; something of his wild-
ness had never died in him. In the Museum at Odense
is a replica of Hans Andersen's last rooms; his walnut
writing-table is there, laid out ready for writing with
pens, blotter, knife, and scissors; his calling cards, let-
tered proudly: "Hans Christian Andersen, Conseiller

d'Etat," are in a drawer. There is the screen he made himself of picture scraps, his jug and basin, his house boots, and his bed, a curiously small bed for such a big man. That bed was the first piece of furniture he had ever owned and it filled him with dismay. He said rebelliously: "If only I were twenty-two again I would take two shirts and a pair of socks, put my quill pen in my pocket, sling an inkwell on my back, and go out into the wide world."

Perhaps it was to get away from the bed that he still traveled; to France, Germany, and his beloved Italy. He made new friends, Björnson the Norwegian poet, Bögh, and a prickly young critic, Brandes. He called on Elizabeth Barrett Browning in Italy and once traveled with the dancer Pepita in a railway carriage. He saw Jenny Lind again. "I heard her singing and it was the same soul, the same fountain of music. Taubert's little song, as formed by her lips, was the song of a jubilating warbling bird; the nightingale cannot whistle like that, the thrush cannot quiver." Her husband greeted Andersen kindly, her little son looked at him with wide eyes, but Andersen was not to be beguiled. "She has left the stage, that is a wrong," he wrote, "it is to give up her mission, the gift God chose for her."

Hans Andersen's sense of God was always unquestioning, simple, and direct. It had a quality that seems completely Danish; no one who has gone into the plain Danish country churches with their whitewashed walls and red-tiled roofs can fail to be struck by the absence of fuss; there is quiet, space almost to bareness, room for

prayer; it seems the simplicity that Christ taught. St.
Knud's, at Odense, is now one of the few whitewashed
cathedrals in the world; it has been called stark, but the
glimmering whiteness of the nave, broken only by the
wrought iron and brass of the hanging lamps, leads
the eye straight to the altar, which, made of gold itself,
has the only stained-glass window in the church rising
high, in resplendent colors of blue and gold, behind it.

In one of the strangest and most beautiful of his
stories, *The Marsh King's Daughter*, Andersen makes
the storks tell the heroine, little Helga, who has grown
careless and proud, the legend of the ostrich: "All the
ostriches had once been very beautiful, with big strong
wings. Then one evening the largest birds in the wood
said to the ostrich: 'Brother, mightn't we, God willing,
fly tomorrow to the river and drink?' And the ostrich
answered: 'I'm willing!' So at dawn they flew off; at
first, high in the air towards the sun, God's eye; all the
time higher and higher, with the ostrich flying on far
ahead of all the others. Proudly it flew towards the light,
trusting in its own strength and not in Him who gave it;
the ostrich wouldn't say 'God willing.' Then the aveng-
ing angel drew aside the veil from the blazing sun, so
that the bird's wings were burnt up in a flash, and it
sank miserably to earth. Ever since then no ostriches
have been able to rise into the air. They stampede in a
panic, rush wildly about, but can never leave the ground.
It is a warning to all of us, whatever we think or do, to
say 'God willing.'" Hans Andersen was like the wise
storks, he never forgot God.

When he was at home in Copenhagen, he still liked,
as in his old penurious days, to eat his dinner at different
houses every day. "Monday calls me to friends of many
years' standing, State Counselor Edvard Collin and his
family; Tuesday takes me to the Drewsens, where Ingeborg is always a steadfast sister to me; on Wednesday to
Örsted's home; he himself is gone, but his wife and
youngest daughter, Mathilde, are still there"—the very
Mathilde whose little first bound edition of the Tales,
green leather with gilt stamping, is in a showcase in the
Odense Museum. Friday was the day for Henriette
Wulff's sister. Thursday used to belong to the old
Collins, but now that day and Saturday had had to find
new friends.

Andersen had met two families, Jewish, cultured,
liberal, and kind, the Henriques and the Melchiors.
Mrs. Henriques was the mother of the adored little
Maria; Dorothea Melchior had been born a Henriques.
In their portraits none of Andersen's friends looks more
attractive; there is a glowing darkness in eyes and hair,
a gentle clever expression that speaks of their quickness of
response, their sensitive kindness. Here, in his home
city, Andersen found the wit, the nobility of feeling,
the knowledge he had come to look for in a Jenny Lind
or his friends abroad. Mrs. Henriques was a musician;
on Sundays he went to her house for music, and both
families took him into their circle and made him an
intimate.

The Collins would once again have looked down

their noses at what the Melchiors and Henriques not only allowed but encouraged; a girl visitor to the Henriques house remarked how Mr. Andersen had all the attention, and had to be served first at table, or he became annoyed. The indulgence was not good for him; when he had been more with the astringent Collins he had written his finest work; with the Henriques and Melchiors, the Tales grew weak; they were charming but had not the crispness of the older ones, except perhaps *Aunty Toothache.*

It was the last he wrote, and he could write only too feelingly about toothache because for years he had suffered gnawing relentless pain. When *The Mulatto* was being written he had lost a tooth and had said: "If only I could have my tooth again, never mind about *The Mulatto,*" and the celebrations at Odense had been marred by toothache.

"Will you acknowledge," says Aunty Toothache, "that I am mightier than poetry, philosophy, mathematics, and all music? Mightier than all the notions that are painted on canvas or carved in marble? I am older than every one of them . . . believe me, there was power in the first toothache."

"I believe it all," said the poet. "But go away! Go away!"

Even toothache could be made into a story; almost to the end, Andersen kept his quick interest in even the most trivial things. "It has just struck me that I can enrich your wife's cookery book," he wrote to Edvard from Le Locle when he was very old. It was a recipe for a salad. "The addition is a garlic. The salad is made as usual, then you take a crust of French bread and rub into it a whole garlic. The bread you put in the salad and a piquant flavor is obtained."

He still made his paper cuts and scrapbooks for the Henriques and Melchior children, still arranged flowers, and he still endlessly read his Tales aloud.

The Hans Andersen statue in the King's Garden is a study of this reading. The Melchiors had raised a subscription for a statue to be put up in honor of Andersen and in record time the lists were filled. He was asked to choose the design himself, but most of the sketches, submitted by different sculptors, irritated him by their pretty sentimentality. "I could not bear to have children climbing on my back or sitting on my lap while I read," he said. It was too delicate a process for that; they had to stand or sit properly, everything had to be in order.

This ceremony, the importance of paying attention and giving due, enhances the telling for children. Andersen understood that very well, and everywhere he went children flocked to see him, brought him wreaths and kisses, wrote to him. Once, when he was talking jokingly to a composer friend about the funeral march that would one day have to be written for him, he said: "Most of the people who walk after me will be children; make the beat keep time with little steps."

In those last years there were more ceremonies, more honors. On the fiftieth anniversary of Andersen's arrival in Copenhagen there was a public banquet, and on his seventieth birthday a wonderful private dinner at the Melchiors'.

Danish people have a talent for parties and celebrations; in the older houses there was a festival room, kept apart and usually larger and more elegantly furnished than the rest; it was opened and decorated for occasions and parties, and what parties they were! The confirmation celebration is a great day, and for silver and golden weddings the house is decorated with flowers and ribbons; the day after a party the hostess is complimented by letters or calls and no one thinks of going to see a bride or a new woman acquaintance without a gift of flowers. Andersen's birthday dinner was a wonderful affair. The menu and list of wines—some of these rather curious—were built round his Tales.

MENU

April 2, 1875

Neighbors	Oysters
Soup from a sausage	
Spin a long yarn about nothing	
From the Barnyard	Turkey
Under the Willow	Champignons
What you can hit on ⎫ *Five from a pea pod* ⎭	Frittered sweetbreads with green peas
Something	Salmon with asparagus

The Top and the Ball
    [*literal translation from
    the Danish = Sweet-
    hearts*]
	Wine jelly

The Wild Swans	Game

Everything in its place
*Ask the old lady from
    Amager*
	Danish open sandwiches,
	    cheese and radishes

The Ice Maiden and the Snowman	Dessert

WINES

SOMETHING FROM THE BOTTLENECK

The Old House	(Château Giraud)
From Spain	(Sherry, Champagne)
The Jumpers	(Champagne)
It's as true as true	(Bordeaux)
The loveliest rose in the world	(Château Larose)
She was good for nothing	(Madeira)
Aunty	(Veuve Cliquot)
Foregone is not forgotten	(Old Madeira)
The Last Pearl	(Malvasier)

"My seventieth birthday was a day rich in sunshine and blessing," Andersen wrote to the editor of the *New York Tribune*, who had sent a gift of books from the

children of America. "From every part of my beloved
motherland and far away beyond its boundaries came
beautiful presents, letters, and telegrams. For what an
infinite amount of goodness I have to be thankful." But
in his letter to the Grand Duke of Weimar, who sent
him a new Order, he said that though it was a great and
splendid day, he was very ill and could hardly receive
the deputations and visitors. "God willing," he said,
I shall soon leave town. Only country quiet and summer
warmth can help me now."

The Melchiors took him to their summer villa,
Rolighed, which means Quietude; it looked over the
blue waters of the Sound and had a garden that stretched
down to the sea; at first Andersen was able to walk about
and sit out in the sun, then he had to stay in bed.

His last work was for a child. Though he was very
weak, he dictated a poem, *Spring in Kjöge*, to Mrs.
Melchior for her little daughter Charlotte; after that he
was silent, only smiling at anyone who helped him or
came near him. Once, when Mrs. Melchior brought him
a white rose, he kissed her hand.

On the 4th of August 1875 Melchior sent a telegram to Edvard; in the showcase at the Odense Museum
the post-office writing on its yellowed sheet is still clear:
"At eleven o'clock this morning, our beloved mutual
friend passed peacefully away."

In Denmark, for a funeral, flowers are strewn up the
aisle of the church; it is as if it were a wedding, a new
beginning.

Hans Andersen is buried in Copenhagen, but people

do not often go to see his grave; they go to the King's Garden to see his reading statue, to the Langelinie to see the Little Mermaid. In Odense the house where he was born has been made into a museum, and so many visitors ask the way to it that the red and white signposts of the city, besides painting the kilometers to Svendborg and Nyborg and Bogense, have an extra arm that reads: *"Til H. C. Andersen's Hus."*

In *The Last Dream of the Oak Tree*, the oak and the mayfly talk of death, when life will be over.

"Over, what is over?" asks the little fly. "Will all the beauty in the world die when you die?" she asks the tree.

"It will last longer, infinitely longer than I am able to imagine," says the great oak tree.

INDEX

This book was set on the Linotype in a face called *El-dorado*, so named by its designer, WILLIAM ADDISON DWIGGINS, as an echo of Spanish adventures in the Western World. The series of experiments that culminated in this type-face began in 1942; the designer was trying a page more "brunette" than the usual book type. "One wanted a face that should be sturdy, and yet not too mechanical. . . . Another desideratum was that the face should be narrowish, compact, and close fitted, for reasons of economy of materials." The specimen that started Dwiggins on his way was a type design used by the Spanish printer A. de Sancha at Madrid about 1774. Eldorado, however, is in no direct way a copy of that letter, though it does reflect the Madrid specimen in the anatomy of its arches, curves, and junctions. Of special interest in the lower-case letters are the stresses of color in the blunt, sturdy serifs, subtly counterbalanced by the emphatic weight of some of the terminal curves and finials. The roman capitals are relatively open, and winged with liberal serifs and an occasional festive touch.

This book was composed, printed, and bound by The Plimpton Press, Norwood, Massachusetts. The typography and binding were designed by the creator of its type-face—W. A. Dwiggins.

WAD